Institute of Leadership
& Management

superseries

Planning to
Work Efficiently

FIFTH EDITION

Published for the
Institute of Leadership & Management

ELSEVIER

AMSTERDAM • BOSTON • HEIDELBERG • LONDON • NEW YORK • OXFORD
PARIS • SAN DIEGO • SAN FRANCISCO • SINGAPORE • SYDNEY • TOKYO
Pergamon Flexible Learning is an imprint of Elsevier

Pergamon
Flexible
Learning

Pergamon Flexible Learning is an imprint of Elsevier
Linacre House, Jordan Hill, Oxford OX2 8DP, UK
30 Corporate Drive, Suite 400, Burlington, MA 01803, USA

First edition 1986
Second edition 1991
Third edition 1997
Fourth edition 2003
Fifth edition 2007

Editor: David Pardey

Based on material in previous editions of this work

The views expressed in this work are those of the authors and do
not necessarily reflect those of the Institute of Leadership &
Management or of the publisher

Notice
No responsibility is assumed by the publisher for any injury and/or damage to persons or
property as a matter of products liability, negligence or otherwise, or from any use or operation
of any methods, products, instructions or ideas contained in the material herein

British Library Cataloguing in Publication Data
A catalogue record for this book is available from the British Library

Library of Congress Cataloguing in Publication Data
A catalogue record for this book is available from the Library of Congress

ISBN: 978-0-08-046421-3

For information on all Pergamon Flexible Learning publications
visit our website at http://books.elsevier.com

Institute of Leadership & Management
Registered Office
1 Giltspur Street
London
EC1A 9DD
Telephone: 020 7294 2470
www.i-l-m.com
ILM is a part of the City & Guilds Group

Typeset by Charon Tec Ltd (A Macmillan Company), Chennai, India
www.charontec.com
Printed and bound in Great Britain

07 08 09 10 11   10 9 8 7 6 5 4 3 2 1

Working together to grow
libraries in developing countries

www.elsevier.com | www.bookaid.org | www.sabre.org

ELSEVIER   BOOK AID
International   Sabre Foundation

Contents

Series preface

Whether you are a tutor/trainer or studying management development to further your career, Super Series provides an exciting and flexible resource to help you to achieve your goals. The fifth edition is completely new and up-to-date, and has been structured to perfectly match the Institute of Leadership & Management (ILM)'s new unit-based qualifications for first line managers. It also harmonizes with the 2004 national occupational standards in management and leadership, providing an invaluable resource for S/NVQs at Level 3 in Management.

Super Series is equally valuable for anyone tutoring or studying any management programmes at this level, whether leading to a qualification or not. Individual workbooks also support short programmes, which may be recognized by ILM as Endorsed or Development Awards, or provide the ideal way to undertake CPD activities.

For learners, coping with all the pressures of today's world, Super Series offers you the flexibility to study at your own pace to fit around your professional and other commitments. You don't need a PC or to attend classes at a specific time – choose when and where to study to suit yourself! And you will always have the complete workbook as a quick reference just when you need it.

For tutors/trainers, Super Series provides an invaluable guide to what needs to be covered, and in what depth. It also allows learners who miss occasional sessions to 'catch up' by dipping into the series.

Super Series provides unrivalled support for all those involved in first line management and supervision.

Unit specification

Title:	Planning to work efficiently		Unit Ref:	M3.20
Level:	3			
Notional credit value:	2	Guided learning hours	10-12 (midpoint 11)	

Learning outcomes *The learner will*	Assessment criteria *The learner can (in an organization with which the learner is familiar)*	
1. Know how to plan work	1.1	Identify targets set for the team; and state indicators to measure performance
	1.2	Use *one* planning technique to plan an appropriate job activity
	1.3	Explain *one* technique to monitor and control a planned job activity
	1.4	Explain the importance of the supply chain in delivering results and meeting customer requirements
2. Understand the importance of efficiency and effectiveness to achieve objectives	2.1	Explain the importance of effectiveness and efficiency to achieve your workplace objectives
	2.2	Explain how efficiency and effectiveness are measured in your organization

Workbook introduction

1 ILM Super Series study links

This workbook addresses the issues of *Planning to Work Efficiently*. Should you wish to extend your study to other Super Series workbooks covering related or different subject areas, you will find a comprehensive list at the back of this book.

2 Links to ILM qualifications

This workbook relates to the learning outcomes of Unit M3.20 Planning to work efficiently from the ILM Level 3 Award, Certificate and Diploma in First Line Management.

3 Links to S/NVQs in Management

This workbook relates to the following Unit of the Management Standards which are used in S/NVQs in Management, as well as a range of other S/NVQs:

D6. Allocate and monitor the progress and quality of work in your area of responsibility

4 Workbook objectives

In 1995 Sir John Harvey-Jones wrote:

> We talk continuously about the need to improve our productivity and, God knows, it is a dire need: yet we appear to accept with equanimity that in the world of work we are achieving less than half our capacity. Luckily for us few other countries do much better, but the potential for improvement is so vast that it is incomprehensible that we do not debate, study and struggle to do better.
> (Source: John Harvey-Jones (1995) *All Together Now*, Mandarin.)

What was true in 1995 is, sadly, still true today. We still have a long way to go before we can say that our businesses run as efficiently as they might.

However, by deciding to study this workbook you have taken the first step towards addressing the problem of planning and controlling your team's work in an efficient and effective manner so that costs are reduced and waste is minimized.

There are four sessions. Session A can be summarized very concisely, as follows:

> Work is about converting resources into outputs. These resources are capital, materials, information, energy, equipment, time, finance and people. It is in the optimum management of resources that efficiency is achieved. The manager desiring improvements in efficiency must therefore identify the resources at his or her command, and find ways of getting the best from them.

As a team leader, you almost certainly make plans every day, and you will no doubt be responsible for monitoring and controlling some of your team's activities. Controlling is a matter of checking on performance, and taking appropriate corrective actions. There are many ways of reaching the same end goal, and what will be right for one team won't suit another; nevertheless, the basic principles of planning and control are widely applicable.

Session B deals with control systems, and then discusses seven stages of controlling work activities, the first two of which are 'Define objectives' and 'Make a plan'.

Session C is mainly about resources: people, materials and equipment. We also look at work methods, work flow and quality.

In Session D, we turn to the planning and control of projects. A project is an undertaking with definite objectives, to be achieved in a limited timescale.

A story which illustrates the distinction between efficiency and effectiveness is that of a surgeon who was said to have improved his efficiency by completing more operations in a day, only to reduce his effectiveness as all his patients died.

Although project management tends to be treated as a specialized subject in many textbooks, the basic approach and techniques can be used in all kinds of situations.

4.1 Objectives

When you have completed this workbook you will be better able to:

- recognize what efficiency means in the context of your workplace;
- identify the stages involved in planning and controlling work, and apply them to your own environment;
- control the resources available to you and your team;
- recognize the importance of setting, and checking against, agreed standards;
- contribute to the planning and control of projects.

5 Activity planner

The following Activities require some planning so you may want to look at these now.

- In Activity 21 you are asked to think about the effectiveness of your methods of communication with the team, and try to find a way in which these methods could be improved.
- Activity 26 asks you to look at the way you make recommendations for improvements to activities, and decide what you will do differently next time.

Both of these Activities may provide the basis of evidence for your S/NVQ portfolio. All Portfolio Activities and the Work-based assignment are sign-posted with this icon.

The icon states the elements to which the Portfolio Activities and Work-based assignment relate.

Session A
Background to efficiency

1 Introduction

One of the great gurus of management theory, Peter Drucker, used to say that the only thing that differentiates one business from another is the quality of its management. And the only way to measure that quality is through a measurement of productivity that shows how well resources are utilized and how much they yield. (Peter F Drucker, *The Practice of Management.*[1])

Managers need to have many qualities, including: industry, honesty, self-confidence, a sense of fairness, moral courage, consistency, audacity. Commendable as these attributes are, they are very difficult to measure, and they don't **necessarily** lead to good results for the organization. Efficiency (or productivity), on the other hand, can usually be calculated, and the efficient manager is recognized as a successful manager.

Taking another view, the work managers do can be said to consist of:

■ achieving desired results by giving direction to others
■ balancing efficiency and effectiveness
■ getting the most from limited resources.

The last two of these are the subjects of this workbook.

This session aims to help you get a good understanding of efficiency and effectiveness at work.

[1] Paperback edition (1989), page 68, Butterworth-Heinemann.

1

2 Work organizations

It can be useful to classify work organizations into four groups or sectors. We have the:

- **manufacturing sector**, where goods are produced
- **transport sector**, in which people or goods are transferred
- **supply sector**, which supplies goods it does not manufacture
- **service sector**, where services, rather than physical goods, are passed to the customer.

Activity 1

2 mins

Which sector or sectors do your employers fall into?

_____

_____

Most organizations are not difficult to categorize. All manufacturers, of whatever commodity, are obviously in the first group. Apart from industrial companies, manufacturing includes agriculture, the construction industry, and the energy producers, i.e. generators of electricity and manufacturers of gas and oil products.

Airlines, bus companies and freight companies are all in the transportation business. Shops, distributors, car dealers and so on fall into the supply sector. The service sector includes such organizations as hairdressers, building societies, restaurants, etc.

Of course, some companies, especially the larger corporations, can claim to be represented in more than one sector. Marks and Spencer plc, for example, supplies clothes and food, and offers financial services. The Virgin group's enterprises include shops (supply), radio broadcasting (service), and an airline (transport). Also, some industries really straddle two sectors: holiday travel companies are not simply in the business of transporting people; their main aim is to offer a service.

Which of these four sectors is the largest?

In many countries, including the UK, the service sector has long since supplanted manufacturing as the largest group, with that trend likely to continue.

You may read or hear people lamenting the 'decline of our great manufacturing industries'. In the United States, the same sentiments are often expressed. These complaints may be justified in the sense that those countries with a strong manufacturing base have traditionally been among the richest. However, there are many who argue that this is less true today. Britain may make fewer cars and tractors than it used to, but it exports a vast range of services which earn a great deal of money and prestige.

Whatever you think about this, you will perhaps agree that it is silly to suggest that one work sector is somehow more 'worthy' than another. Real work is done in all organizations.

But we are getting away from our subject. Let's now turn to the question of what work itself consists of.

3 Work as a transforming process

When we do work on something, we change it in some way. A wood-turner takes a piece of wood and (literally) turns it into a chair leg; a skilled gardener can transform a plot of rough ground into a delight to the eye by filling it with flowers and shrubs; a builder changes bricks and mortar into houses. Another way of putting it is to say that all work is a **transforming** process.

Thus we can say that work organizations of all kinds carry out transformations. In its simplest form, the work process is shown by the following diagram:

Transformations consist of one or more of three types:

- improving
- caretaking
- transferring.

The simplest examples to identify are those in the manufacturing sector. A power station has inputs of water plus coal, oil or nuclear fuel, and it 'improves' these inputs first to steam and then to electricity, its final output. Textile mills transform fibres into cloth. To 'improve' is another way of saying 'add value to'.

The inputs and outputs of a school happen to be the same: children. The transformations taking place here are those of caretaking – safeguarding through a period of time, and improving – increasing the children's knowledge and understanding.

What about transferring? We can say that a taxi company 'transforms' people by transferring them to their desired destination, while taking care of them during the journey. A waste disposal company is also in the business of transferring and caretaking.

Activity 2

Jot down the inputs, transformation processes and outputs of your own organization (or, if there are many, **three** or **four** of them).

Inputs   Transformation type   Outputs

_____   _____   _____

_____   _____   _____

_____   _____   _____

_____   _____   _____

In case you had difficulty with this, here are a few more examples.

An airline transfers people from one place to another (movement in space), while taking care of them through time, and (conceivably) 'improving' them by making them more rested, or better fed.

A chiropodist improves people by attending to their feet. Financial advisers have as their inputs the financial affairs of their clients, which they aim to improve by proposing sound investments. A baker converts flour and yeast into bread and cakes. Farmers take as inputs seeds, soil and fertilizers in order to produce outputs of crops. The inputs of beauticians could be said to be the faces and bodies of their customers, which they try to improve by making them more beautiful.

Operations management is defined in the book of the same name by John Naylor as follows:

> Operations management is concerned with creating, operating and controlling a transformation system which takes inputs of a variety of resources and produces outputs of goods and services which are needed by customers.

EXTENSION 1
Introduction to Operations Management, John Naylor. Most of the topics covered in this workbook are typically included under the general topic area of **operations management.**

4 Introduction to resources

The inputs to work processes are called **resources**, which can be classified in at least three ways. You may see resources separated into:

- **m**oney
- **m**anpower
- **m**achines and
- **m**aterials

– the four Ms.

A second classification is 'land, capital and labour'. Here, land is the term used to describe all natural resources, including water, airspace and raw materials. Capital is all non-human, non-natural resources, and labour is the term used for human resources.

However, the most usual way of categorizing resources, and the one we will use, is:

- people
- capital
- materials
- information.

Let's look at what we mean by these four groups.

- **People** (also called **labour**): those who run the organization, and work in it

It should be said from the start that many object to applying the word 'resource' to people.

It does seem strange and unfeeling to think of people as a resource. We do this simply for convenience. But it is important to remember, when bracketing employees alongside capital, materials and information, that:

people are the most precious, most flexible and most necessary of all the resources of an organization.

Without people to organize and direct the work, nothing worthwhile can be achieved, even in those workplaces where there is a high level of automation.

Getting the best from people, whether or not you classify them as a resource, is the most challenging aspect of a manager's job.

- **Capital**: equipment, machinery, finance, land, buildings and goodwill

  We define capital as the permanent or semi-permanent assets of the organization, apart from people, which are needed to enable goods and services to be produced.

  Deciding how equipment, finance, land, buildings and goodwill can be used to best effect occupies much of the time and efforts of management.

- **Materials**: raw materials and components, which are converted or consumed by the process, together with the energy consumed

  These are the direct inputs: the ingredients which are used up in producing the goods or services that are the outputs of an organization.

  Frequently, this is the group of resources where the most waste occurs, and which consequently has the greatest potential for savings and improved efficiency.

- **Information**: a vital resource, which includes the know-how to do the work, knowledge of competitors and markets, and so on

  No work can be done without intelligence. Often, it is the best informed managers who are the most effective and efficient.

  Time is sometimes listed as a separate resource, and is certainly a constraining factor in all human endeavour.

  It is difficult to think of an organization which can operate without every one of these resources. Our model can therefore be modified to:

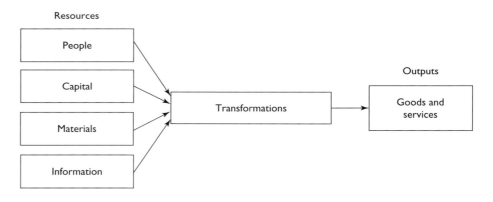

Activity 3 · 3 mins

Now think about your own organization again, and list a few of its resources as people, capital, materials and information. Jot down just **three** examples of each type.

People: _____

Capital: _____

Materials: _____

Information: _____

Answers to this Activity can be found on page 117.

We need to go on to discuss resources in more detail, but before doing that, we should return to our main theme: efficiency and effectiveness.

5 Efficiency

By defining exactly what we mean by efficiency and effectiveness, we will have a better idea of how resources can be used efficiently and effectively.

Activity 4 · 3 mins

How would you define the word 'efficiency'?

_____

_____

_____

There are several ways to express what efficiency means; compare your answer with the following. Efficiency has been defined as:

- ■ 'a measure of how well resources are transformed into outputs'
- ■ 'working well with little waste'
- ■ 'getting the most out of what you put in'
- ■ 'the production of the maximum result from the minimum effort'
- ■ 'the best use of resources to achieve production of goods or services'.

The last definition is the one most meaningful in the context of this work-book. To be efficient, we must make the best use of resources, that is, we have to find ways of utilizing resources to produce the goods or services we want, with the minimum of waste. To repeat the definition:

Efficiency means making the best use of resources in achieving production of goods or services.

The main purpose of the workbook is to investigate ways in which this can be done. Relevant activities in achieving efficiency at work are likely to include:

- developing existing resources
- reducing the amount or cost of resources
- utilizing existing resources in the best way
- finding better resources than the ones we have
- minimizing waste.

5.1 Why is efficiency important?

It may seem obvious to say that all organizations want to be more efficient. But why? What is the effect of increased efficiency? So far as any commercial company is concerned, the answer can be summed up in the following diagram:

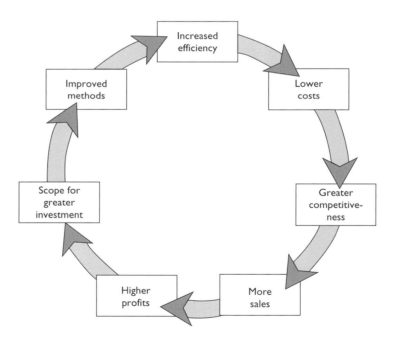

As you can see, the effects are self-regenerating. As efficiency increases, so costs go down, and the organization has leeway to reduce prices, resulting in enhanced competitiveness. This leads to higher sales and profits, and opens the way for the organization to invest in even better methods of production. Efficiency can then be raised even more, and the cycle continues.

5.2 Efficiency and control

At each point of the cycle there must be an element of control. Without control it will be difficult to gauge how efficient the organization is becoming, or where changes in performance are proving as efficient as required. All managers will recognize that their role includes a degree of control, particularly in relation to the use of the organization's resources.

Control will result in:

- planning processes which are more likely to succeed
- achievement of objectives
- identification and use of resources which are of the correct quality and quantity
- ability to take appropriate corrective action – less reactive, more proactive response to problems
- improved forecasting and estimating
- thorough assessment of performance, enabling constructive feedback and improved staff performance overall.

Activity 5

5 mins

What day-to-day methods of control do you use, and how do they contribute to efficient working?

_____

_____

_____

Methods and types of control will vary between organizations, but essentially they will have a similar purpose – to ensure that working practices result in the organization achieving its objectives and enhancing its performance.

5.3 Balancing efficiency with effectiveness

Peter Drucker described efficiency as 'doing things right', and effectiveness as 'doing the right things'.

Effectiveness has also been defined as:

- ■ 'an assessment of how far a stated objective is achieved'
- ■ 'being concerned with the achievement of set organizational goals or objectives'.

There is an important distinction between efficiency and effectiveness. It is perfectly possible to be efficient and yet ineffective, as you read in the Workbook introduction. The jeweller who saves on materials while producing brooches that no one wants to wear can hardly claim to have attained her objectives.

Objectives are the prime driver in terms of effectiveness and efficiency. It will always be possible for someone to achieve objectives where every conceivable resource is made available. In this case the jeweller can be argued to have been effective – she achieved her objective. However this is not efficient because, as we have already learned, **efficiency means making the best use of resources**.

Balancing effectiveness and efficiency is part of the managerial role, and will require you as a manager in using the most appropriate methods and types of control available to you.

It is most likely that the objectives of your organization will include reference to its customers – the people to which it provides goods and services.

Work team objectives are typically expanded versions of the following:

'We aim to provide a first class service (or high quality goods) to our customers, in an efficient manner.'

Your customers may be another team, or they may be the customers of the organization itself.

All commercial enterprises must ultimately direct their activities towards satisfying their customers. Even non-commercial organizations, such as charities and schools, can be said to have customers. So our earlier model of work organizations should be modified just once more to give:

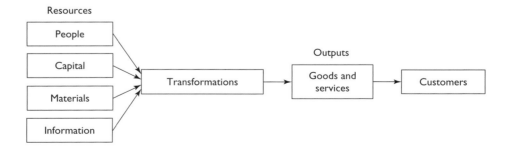

Work organizations transform resources (capital, materials and information, with the help of people) into goods and services, which are provided to their customers.

This model can help us identify sources of inefficiency and ineffectiveness.

Activity 6 · 10 mins

Examine the *Resources:Transformations:Outputs:Customers* model.

Try to identify two potential examples of **inefficiency**. Describe where within the model they might occur, and what the impact might be at later stages. One example might be having the wrong quality of materials, which will result in customer dissatisfaction later in the model.

_____

_____

Now, try to identify two potential examples of **ineffectiveness**. Again, describe where within the model they might occur, and what the impact might be at later stages. You could say, for example, producing a product which has no customers willing to buy it.

_____

_____

The answer to this question can be found on page 117.

Here are some further examples of inefficiency and ineffectiveness.

A manicurist could be inefficient by wasting materials, turning up late for appointments, and so on. Ineffectiveness might presumably be accomplished by breaking the clients' nails.

If a school canteen were to spoil food, it would be less than fully efficient. But if it were to cook insufficient meals for the number of children to be served, so that some went hungry, it would be less than fully effective.

In a similar way, a bricklayer who damaged new bricks might be called inefficient. Building a crooked wall, though, should cause the bricklayer to be labelled both ineffective (in not achieving the aim of building a straight wall), *and* inefficient (in thereby causing the wall to have to be built again).

If we want to be efficient and effective, we have to find ways of doing the opposite kinds of things from those mentioned above.

The concept of effectiveness is relevant to all jobs, and efficiency is relevant to nearly all, no matter what products or services are provided by the organization.

6 Quality

There's one other very relevant topic worth taking a look at before getting back to the subject of resources, and that is 'quality'.

Activity 7 · 4 mins

How would you define 'high quality'? Try to sum up the meaning of these words in a couple of sentences. You could, for example, start by thinking about what you mean by high quality as a customer, when you buy something in a shop.

_____

_____

_____

_____

You might say that high quality means:

- getting the kind of products and services that you want
- conforming to a high standard
- the best there is
- excellence.

These are all correct, so far as they go.

When we want to buy something – whether it is food, clothing, luxury items or any other product – we usually have a good deal of choice. There may be a number of different shops and outlets selling goods made by a number of different manufacturers.

Because of all this choice, the goods and services which best meet the needs of customers will sell well. The goods and services which fail to provide customers with what they want will not sell so well – or may not sell at all.

Quality is in fact concerned with **every** aspect of a product.

Quality can be defined as all the features and characteristics of a product or service which affect its ability to satisfy the needs of customers and users.

This definition provides a clue to the link between efficiency, effectiveness and quality. We have already agreed that effectiveness means the achievement of objectives, and that the objectives of all commercial organizations are inevitably linked to satisfying customers.

It is the most effective organizations that are best able to achieve high standards of quality, by delivering the products and services that their customers want. And it is the most efficient ones that are able to survive and prosper in competitive markets.

We will not dwell further on quality in this workbook. You will find more information on this subject in *Providing Quality to Customers* in this series.

However, before we move on, it is worth mentioning 'the **five rights of customers**'. These are the aspects of quality that every customer has a right to expect. They are:

- the right product or service
- of the right quality
- at the right time
- in the right place
- at the right price.

Only when a commercial organization consistently delivers products or services which meet these expectations can it say that it is being fully effective in its objectives in satisfying its customers.

In the next five sections, we return to the subject of resources.

7 People as a resource

On page 5 we listed the resources which are inputs to the work process. They are:

- people
- capital
- materials
- information.

Let's look at people first.

Activity 8 · 15 mins

Read the following statements carefully, and comment upon them. In each case, tick the appropriate box to indicate whether you think it is, in your experience, 'accurate', 'partially accurate' or 'inaccurate'. Then write a sentence or two explaining the reason for your choice. Think about your own organization as you answer.

	Accurate	Partially accurate	Inaccurate

I think the employees of an organization are typically:

a an underdeveloped resource; ☐ ☐ ☐

because _____

_____

b more caring about, and interested in, their work ☐ ☐ ☐
than most employers recognize;

because _____

_____

c an undervalued resource; ☐ ☐ ☐

because _____

_____

d treated as if they could easily be replaced; ☐ ☐ ☐

because _____

_____

e less efficient or reliable than machines; ☐ ☐ ☐

because _____

_____

f the most adaptable, precious and potentially useful ☐ ☐ ☐
resource the organization has;

because _____

_____

Your views on these statements are as valid as the next person's. There are no right or wrong answers. Compare your response with the following points.

a There seems to be little doubt that, in many organizations, people are an underdeveloped resource. You may feel that you, or other members of your team, are not being given the opportunities to use your abilities to the full. Most employers create and define jobs, and then try to find the people to fill them. This is inevitably a difficult matching process. While many employees find themselves capable of fulfilling their assigned roles, they may in truth not feel well suited to the job they are made to do.

In smaller organizations, and in some enlightened larger ones, the task may be moulded to the individual, rather than the other way round. The question changes from one of 'What should the person in this job be doing?' to 'What are we as individuals capable of, and how can our combined skills be used to achieve our objectives?' This approach gives people greater scope for self-expression and development.

b A related question is that of whether employees are more caring about, and interested in, their work than most employers recognize. Again, your response will reflect your experience and point of view; it depends on the people, and on the employer. Most people do care about their jobs, and would be willing to contribute more, given some encouragement.

c,d Are employees an undervalued resource? This is perhaps a more debatable point. If you decided that this statement is accurate, it may be that you feel undervalued yourself, or have seen organizations or executives who treat their workers with scant regard.

Certainly, when so many people have lost their jobs in recent years (said to be over 5 million employees in the 1990s in the UK alone), an unbiased observer might think that employees are often treated as if they were expendable. 'Cost cutting' and 'improvements in efficiency' can sometimes seem to be an excuse for organizations to lay off staff.

e   Are people less efficient or less reliable than machines? Perhaps you will agree that there is some truth in this. When it comes to performing routine tasks repetitively, there is no contest: automated processes win easily. But the time has not yet come when machines can truly 'think'. We have not yet seen a factory where the intelligence and thinking efficiency of people is not needed. (However, who can say this will never happen?)

People at work do get replaced by machines, and the justification is usually an economic one. However, you don't *necessarily* increase efficiency simply by introducing more equipment; every case has to be considered on its merits.

f   You will perhaps agree that this last statement is accurate. Employees are the most adaptable, precious and potentially useful resource the organization has.

As we will discuss later in the workbook, an important approach to achieving improvements in efficiency is to find ways of getting the best from your team.

8 Capital as a resource

8.1 Land and buildings

The land and buildings of an organization, assuming they are owned outright, are usually among its most valuable assets. It goes without saying, therefore, that they should be used efficiently and effectively.

Activity 9 · 3 mins

What do you think is entailed in making effective and efficient use of land and buildings? Try to list **two** things.

_____

_____

_____

Some points you may have mentioned are that buildings and land should be:

- maintained properly, so that they retain their value
- allocated between people, sections and departments so that each group has the right amount of space and facilities, in the right location
- developed to their full potential; for example, an old building may need to be demolished and replaced (subject to current planning regulations) if it no longer serves the needs of the organization adequately.

8.2 Finance

By finance, we mean funds (i.e. available money) or the provision of funds. Of course, buildings, land and other resources are valuable, but they would first have to be sold before they could be used to purchase other things.

> Budgets are itemized summaries of expected income and expenditure over a period.

Unless you work in the finance department of your organization, the primary way in which you help to control finance will probably be through **budgets**.

Give some thought to the following questions. You may not feel you can write down answers straight away; if you can't, keep the questions in mind as you go about your work in the next few days.

Activity 10

How could you keep the finance you are responsible for under better control?

_____

_____

_____

What further information, if any, would help you do this?

_____

_____

_____

8.3 Equipment

Equipment and machinery are the tools of work, and may include items as diverse as screwdrivers, computers, knitting needles, ovens, sewing machines and welding gear. Often, machinery is both expensive and complicated, and requires a good deal of understanding if it is to be used efficiently. As with other assets, a proper schedule of maintenance is usually necessary.

8.4 Goodwill

The capital of an organization includes intangible items that are sometimes difficult to put a value on. Probably the most important of these is **goodwill**.

Activity 11

Explain briefly what you understand by the term 'goodwill'.

_____

_____

_____

How might goodwill be lost, and what will be the effects if it is lost?

_____

_____

_____

As you might have said, the goodwill of an organization is the value of how it is seen by others – its good reputation. Goodwill has real worth, which can be realized when the organization is sold.

Goodwill may be lost by, for example:

- delivering poor quality goods or services to customers
- dealing with customers in an high-handed fashion

- failing to address complaints or concerns expressed by members of the public
- having poor relations with the press
- having an uncaring attitude to the environment.

In the case of commercial companies, the effects of lost goodwill are, sooner or later, loss of profits resulting from lost sales.

Loss of goodwill comes about through ineffectiveness or inefficiency, and leads to reduced profits.

9 Materials as a resource

Material resources are those things consumed (energy and consumable items) or converted (raw materials and components) during the work process.

For example, hospitals consume hypodermic needless, drugs, bandages, and blood and convert sick people to well ones; printers consume ink and convert blank paper to printed copy; poachers consume shot-gun pellets and convert live animals to dead ones; laundries consume washing powder and water and convert dirty washing to clean.

If you can save on materials you will automatically become more efficient.

Activity 12

From your own work area give two examples each of:

- consumed material resources
- converted material resources

_____

_____

_____

_____

10 Information as a resource

Although people may complain that there is ineffective or inefficient communication within their organization this is rarely because there is insufficient information. Generally speaking there is more than enough information made available to us every day. We are bombarded with images, ideas, suggestions and news.

For information to be a valid and reliable resource it should be:

- accurate and complete
- sufficient and available at a time when it can support decision-making and problem-solving processes
- formatted in a way which suits the needs of the recipient, for example paper-based or electronic
- easy to access and retrieve.

Activity 13

15 mins

Identify three items of information which are essential to the work processes in your area of responsibility. For each of these briefly explain:

- where/who it comes from
- how you receive the information
- what you use it for
- any problems you have experienced in relation to this information (consider the list above) and possible ways of solving them.

1 _____

_____

_____

_____

2 _____

_____

_____

_____

3 _____
_____
_____
_____
_____

This Activity should have helped you to realize how important information is in your every day working life. It should also have enabled you to identify problem areas and possible solutions.

● 11 Time as a resource

Time is not always regarded as a separate resource because it is assumed to be part of the use of people. It is so important, however, that it is worth separate consideration here.

Sometimes, saving time can lead directly to increased efficiency. The rule is simple and fairly obvious: if you can perform a task more quickly **without increasing your use of other resources**, then you have improved efficiency. If this is not the case, then the saving in time must be balanced against any extra costs involved.

Self-assessment 1

1 Complete the following diagram, by writing in the correct words:

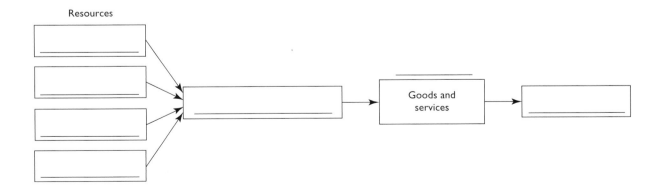

Resources

Goods and services

2   Place the following types of work organization in the most appropriate cells in the table:

   a A UK regional electricity company.
   b A UK water company.
   c A hairdresser.
   d A hardware shop.
   e A residential school.
   f A farm.

Transformation type	Sector			
	Manufacturing	Transport	Supply	Service
Improving				
Caretaking				
Transferring				

3   Complete the following statements by replacing the blanks with suitable words:

   a _____ means making the best use of _____, to achieve production of goods or _____.

   b Work organizations _____ resources (capital, materials and _____, with the help of _____) into goods and services, which are provided to their _____.

   c _____ can be defined as all the _____ and characteristics of a product or service that affect its ability to _____ the needs of customers and _____.

   d For information to be valid and reliable it must be _____ and complete.

4   Suggest two benefits to an organization that can arise as the result of control.

   Answers to these questions can be found on pages 113–14.

12 Summary

- Work organizations can be categorized into four sectors: manufacturing; transport; supply; service.

- Work can be described as a transforming process; transformations may consist of improving, caretaking or transferring.

- Resources are the inputs to the work process, and may be listed as people, capital, materials and information.

- Efficiency means making the best use of resources, to achieve production of goods or services.

- Effectiveness is concerned with the achievement of organizational goals or objectives.

- It is the most effective organizations who are best able to achieve high standards of quality, by delivering the products and services that their customers want. And it is the most efficient ones who are able to survive and prosper in competitive markets.

- People are the most adaptable, precious and potentially useful resource an organization has.

- The land and buildings of an organization, assuming they are owned outright, are usually among its most valuable assets, and therefore should be used efficiently and effectively.

- By finance, we mean funds (i.e. available money) or the provision of funds.

- Often, equipment is both expensive and complicated, and requires a good deal of understanding.

- The goodwill of an organization can be described as the value of how it is seen by others. It is lost through inefficiency or ineffectiveness.

- If you can save on materials, you will automatically become more efficient.

- Materials come in two forms: those that are consumed and those that are converted.

- Every manager can contribute to energy savings.

- Information must be valid and reliable if it is to be a useful resource.

- If you can perform a task quicker without increasing your use of other resources, then you will have improved efficiency.

Session B
Planning and controlling work processes

1 Introduction

> 'Planning is the activity of bridging the gap mentally from where you and the group are now to where you want to be at some future moment in terms of accomplishing a task. The planning function is the response to the group's need: 'How are we going to achieve the task?' But the 'how' question soon leads you to ask also 'who does what?' and 'when does it have be done?' . . . Usually if a plan proves to be inadequate, it is because either you as the leader or the group (or both) have not pressed home these questions until you have clear and definite answers.'
>
> John Adair, *Effective Leadership*[1]

When plans go wrong, we have only ourselves to blame. And when work processes go out of control, it is usually because insufficient time and effort has been spent on the initial planning stage.

This session examines both control and planning systems, and attempts to set out guidelines that will be useful in real-life work situations.

[1] Published by Pan Macmillan, 1988.

2 Control systems

We begin with a little control systems theory, and go on to look at a model for planning and controlling.

2.1 Open and closed loops

Imagine you want to toast a slice of bread in an automatic electric toaster. You place the bread in the toaster and push down the lever. A few minutes later the toast pops up.

Activity 14 · 2 mins

Once you've placed the bread in the toaster and pressed the lever down, how much control do you have over how brown the toast is?

_____

_____

Normally, there is an adjustment you can make to the toaster **before** you put the bread in, which determines how long the heater will stay on. Short of forcing the lever up before the completion of the toasting operation however, **you have no control** over how brown the toast will be once you start. Also, the toaster does not measure 'brownness', and probably will even continue to work if you forget to put the bread in.

This is an example of an **open loop system** – for reasons which will become obvious in a moment.

We can draw a very simple diagram of this toasting process.

Input: bread → | Toasting process | → Output: toast

This is easily made into a more general diagram, which could be applied to any other open loop system:

Now imagine you are taking a shower. Your immediate aim in this case is to get the water to fall on you at a pleasant temperature. You do this by monitoring (feeling) the temperature, and then adjusting the taps. In this case **you do have control** over the temperature of the water.

The diagram for the shower shows this monitoring and adjustment.

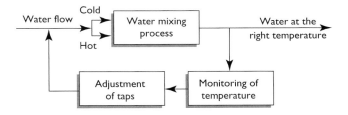

The water coming out of the shower is monitored, and an adjustment made to the taps, to get it to the desired temperature.

The shower is an example of a **closed loop system**.

This illustration can be made into a more general diagram.

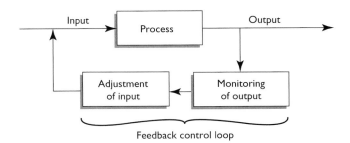

You will see that the 'monitoring' and 'adjustment' components are called the **feedback control loop**. Some part of the output is **fed back** and used to modify the input. It is this feedback control loop that marks the difference between open loop systems and closed loop systems.

Closed loop systems have feedback, monitoring and control. Open loop systems do not.

In this workbook, we are concerned with management control. A management control system operates in the same way as any other closed loop system.

Plans are made for a process to be set in place, and the manager has then to monitor the results, if necessary modifying the process to keep it on the right track.

But before we leave our diagrams of closed loop systems, there is one more element to be included.

2.2 Comparing with a standard

Going back to the shower system, the output was 'water at the right temperature'. But how do we know what is the right temperature?

Or, to take another example, when we drive a car, we try to keep going down the road in a straight line. But what do we mean by 'straight'?

Activity 15

4 mins

When you set up a work process, you may give instructions to your team, provide them with resources (such as a workspace, equipment and materials), and allow them to start work.

Think about any task that has to be accomplished in your own team's work. You probably 'keep an eye on things', at least to begin with, to make sure they're going well. But, having observed what's going on, how do you know, in general terms, whether or not things are progressing satisfactorily?

_____

_____

_____

_____

_____

_____

Perhaps your response was along the lines of: 'Through experience, I've got a clear idea of what I would like to see happening' or 'The standards of work are clearly laid down'.

To control something, you need to have some way of knowing when the process is going as you want it to. The way you do this is to **compare** results and performance against a **standard**. This standard may be in your head, or it may be a measurable quantity. But unless you have a standard, you can't control anything.

One more modification to our diagram shows this.

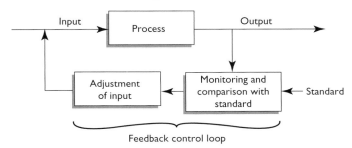

This kind of diagram is only intended to help us recognize that all control systems are the same, whether in management, engineering, or any other human activity. The important point to remember is that:

all systems are controlled by setting a desired standard, and comparing results against this standard.

3 Stages in control

Now let's move on from theoretical control systems to the real-life control of work.

Activity 16

One Monday morning Sanjay, an office supervisor, has the task of getting 20,000 customer information packs collated, individually addressed, checked, sealed in envelopes, and posted by Friday afternoon.

Sanjay starts out well. He makes well-defined plans for the task, and sets up schedules for each part of the work. He assigns four members of staff to the job, and gives them clear instructions. The work will be carried out according to previously defined rules and standards, and with the aid of some automatic equipment.

Sanjay feels confident that he has done all he can to get the job rolling, and so he leaves his team to it.

As the days go by, Sanjay is aware that the 'pack team' is busily working away. Then Friday comes and Sanjay suddenly realizes that only around 13,000 packs have gone out. He has no alternative but to authorize overtime for Friday evening and Saturday so as to get the remaining packs in the post – albeit a day late.

If you had been in Sanjay's shoes, and bearing in mind the control systems we have been looking into, what would you have done to make sure that the job was completed on time? Jot down **two** suggestions.

_____

_____

_____

_____

You may have thought of a number of different ways of tackling this problem.

Referring back to our discussion on systems, we can see that the input to this 'process' was the 20,000 packs that have to be prepared. The desired output is the completion of the work to the required standard, on time.

Sanjay thinks he has worked out what is needed for the wanted result to be achieved automatically. But he has either forgotten that control means **monitoring** what is going on, or he has mistakenly decided that monitoring wasn't necessary. Putting everything in place and pressing the lever is not enough.

Sanjay knew that everyone was busy, but he didn't keep an eye on the rate at which the job was being done. If he had, he could, if necessary, have modified his original plan during the week.

For instance, if he had noted by Wednesday lunchtime that only a third of the packs had gone out, yet that half the time had passed, he might have tried to speed things up by bringing in another staff member.

This case incident illustrates the stages required in controlling work. They are:

- defining your **objectives**;
- making a **plan**;
- **communicating** with the team so that each team member knows the part he or she has to play;

- setting performance **standards**;
- **collecting data** to measure progress;
- **comparing results** with standards and objectives; ⎫
- taking corrective action, and **modifying plans**, ⎬ This is the
  if necessary, to meet objectives. ⎭ monitoring process

The following diagram sums up these points.

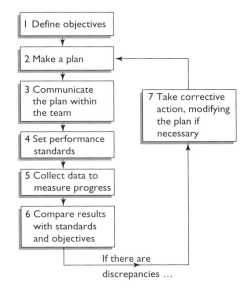

Now, let's look at each of these stages in more detail.

3.1 Defining objectives

Most people would agree that, if you don't know where you are going, you won't know when you get there, and you won't be able to choose the best way of travelling. So when you carry out any sort of planning – whether it is reorganizing the railways or making a cup of tea – you need to have a clear idea of where you want to end up. In planning terms this idea is called an 'objective' or 'goal'.

Objectives vary in detail, depending on who is going to use them. This is illustrated in the diagram below.

At the very top of the objective tree there is often a mission statement which most organizations publish as an expression of their ideals and ambitions. For example, the mission of the University of Cambridge is 'To contribute to society through the pursuit of education, learning, and research at the highest international levels of excellence'.

Below the mission statement, objectives get more practical. There are three levels, each one covering the same area of activity as the one above it, but at a more detailed level. They are:

- organizational objectives;
- project (or team) objectives;
- task objectives.

Organizational objectives. These are general statements of the long-term goals of the whole organization. For example 'To provide an efficient service for all claimants at the benefits office.' or 'To maintain all corporation parks and gardens to a high standard, for the benefit of the public.'

Project (or team) objectives. These are also general in subject matter but relate more to the medium term. They describe the goals set for a particular project or team, and will often have a time limit. Examples would be 'To train new call centre recruits in customer care' or 'To develop a new computer system to enable tennis court bookings to be made online.'

Task objectives. These are short-term and are more detailed than project or team objectives, being focused on specific tasks to be carried out within the project or team. For example 'Within the next 5 days, to write a piece of computer code that will allow a call centre operator to accurately record an electricity meter reading in the customer billing system.'

Finally, you will probably come across one other category of objectives – **performance objectives**. These are statements of personal goals set down for each member of the team or project, usually during a job review. They clarify what is expected of each person in terms of quality, standards of performance and personal development. Performance objectives are discussed in detail in another workbook, *Motivating to Perform*.

Activity 17

5 mins

Jot down the general longer-term objectives of your team. If they have never been written down, you may want to think about what they should be.

A good starting point might be to write down what you think the team's overall function is.

_____

_____

_____

_____

_____

_____

It is important that you know your team objectives and can define them. If you aren't sure what they are, it may be a good idea to discuss the subject with your manager, or talk them over with your team.

The higher-level objectives are very general in the way they describe what has to be achieved, but they are not much help in getting a particular job done. So, if you are given the objective 'To develop a new computer program to enable tennis court bookings to be made online', you will not be any clearer about:

- what exactly you are expected to do;
- what standards you have to achieve;
- what your priorities should be;
- what resources will be needed (this covers everything from desks and pens, to people to do the job);
- what skills you will need;
- when it has to be completed.

So the bottom level of objectives (task objectives) have to be much more specific, with all these details agreed before any work can start.

To be useful these **specific objectives** must be SMART.

S pecific – Clearly describing the desired end result, and addressed to the person who is going to carry the task out.

M easurable – Capable of being measured, that is stating the standards of performance required and the conditions under which the task is to be completed.

A chievable – Realistic and achievable, given the resources available, by the person carrying out the task.

R elevant – Related to the job and relevant to the overall general objective of the project, team or organization.

T ime bound – Containing a time limit by which the task must be completed.

An example of a SMART objective would be as follows.

'By 20 July to publish a newsletter of 10 pages for the local football supporters' club that lists the club's social events for next season.'

Activity 18 · 4 mins

Which of the following do you think are good specific objectives?

a To produce a set of accounts for P Hennessy Ltd by 31 May from records provided by them.
b To write a speech lasting 30 minutes for the Archery Club meeting next Saturday.
c By 31 August, to have sold 40 top-of-the-range washing machines from the York warehouse.
d To interview each member of the team in order to identify their current IT skills and discuss any further training they would like to have.

c is the only effective objective. It is specific, measurable, achievable, related to the job and has a clear time limit.

a is not measurable because it does not give enough information about the contents, layout, etc., to know whether the accounts are of the required standard.

b is not sufficiently specific – it doesn't indicate the subject of the speech.

d does not contain a time limit for the task.

So objectives may be either general (relating to the overall organization, project or team) or specific (relating to the task).

In the case of Sanjay, the office supervisor, his general objective might have been 'To provide an efficient and effective clerical and administrative service to all departments', while one of his specific objectives might have been 'To ensure that 20,000 customer information packs are correctly prepared, checked and posted by Friday afternoon.'

Having clear objectives is necessary for good control.

If your line manager presents you with an overall general objective relating to a group of tasks to be carried out by you and your team, you will have to devise specific objectives for carrying out those tasks.

But you need your team members to 'buy in' to the idea, so the next step is to **negotiate** and **agree** each specific task objective with the member of your team who will carry it out. The result will be that he or she will take owner-ship of the task and feel responsible for making it succeed.

The purpose of negotiating is for you to make sure that the team member:

- is clear about his or her role;
- knows who is responsible for what;
- understands what the required standards are;
- feels able to meet the required standard;
- knows what resources are available;
- knows what the deadlines are;
- understands the order in which tasks are to be done;
- is motivated.

If you discuss all these points with your team members, you are giving them the opportunity to ask questions and mention anything they are worried about. Once all this has been discussed and agreed, everyone is much more likely to feel really involved.

Activity 19

Next time you ask members of your team to carry out a task, make sure that you discuss with them each of the above aspects of the job. Then watch the way they go about the job. Are they any more motivated? Are they more eager to keep you up-to-date about their progress? Does the work go more smoothly?

3.2 Making plans

It may well be part of your job to translate objectives into plans.

A plan is a detailed scheme for attaining an overall general objective, and usu-ally includes a description of the method to be used for carrying out the work.

Before the plan can be drawn up, the general objective must be broken down into specific objectives. These are then entered into the plan together with the following details for each specific objective.

- **What**, exactly, is to be done.
- **Why** the work is being done: for whose benefit.

- **Who** is to do each part of the work.
- **How** it is to be done: the approach, processes, and techniques to be used.
- **When** the work is to be started and completed, and perhaps dates for agreed 'milestones' while the project is in progress.
- **Where** it is to be done.

The plan may be continuous: if you supervise a team of trained librarians your plan for running a library may not alter very much from one month to the next.

On the other hand, the plan may be detailed, and designed to deal with a special set of circumstances, such as a spate of machine failures, or a possible major accident.

The big mistake is to assume that you don't need a plan, because you think the what, why, who, how, when and where are all too self-evident.

In general, plans need to:

- cover all the people within your area of responsibility;
- be realistic and achievable, within the constraints imposed by your organization;
- take account of the abilities of your team, and their need to develop their skills.

Of course, you don't expect to have to draw up detailed schedules for every little job, or to hold endless discussions about trivial tasks. If your team perform much the same kind of work repeatedly, you may only need to be concerned about any new or unusual aspects: new team members, different circumstances, or tight time limits, say. Your plans in this kind of situation may not be written down, but they're well understood. The main danger here is that complacency or boredom will cause standards and quality to fall.

But for anything that's not routine, it is a good idea to write the plan down, and to make sure you have considered every aspect.

> Even if **you** are clear about every aspect of the job, can you be sure that your team are equally confident and positive?

3.3 Communicating your plan

We will look at the planning process again in Session D. For now, let's go on to consider the communication of the plan within the team.

> 2 Make a plan
>
> 3 Communicate the plan within the team
>
> 4 Set performance

Activity 20

6 mins

If you run a work team, you probably use a variety of ways of communicating plans to your team. Indicate below whether you apply each of the methods listed. Then describe the circumstances in which each method might be appropriate.

a Pass on the general objectives, and let the team members get on with it.   ☐

_____

_____

b Make a rough plan to meet the objectives, and let the team members work out the details for themselves.   ☐

_____

_____

c Make detailed plans, and give very specific instructions to each team member.   ☐

_____

_____

There are no wrong answers here. How you set your team to work will depend very much on your style of management, the skills the team members have and the kind of work you do.

Inexperienced people will obviously need to be given more specific information and guidance than those who have done the same job for years.

The amount of detail, and the level and pace at which the plans are communicated, will need to be appropriate for the person concerned.

The key word here is **communication**. Note that communication is a two-way process, and implies information going in **both** directions: listening as well as talking, for example. As a good manager, you will know that it's not enough to say your piece and walk away; you will need to confirm that team members have understood you. This understanding may have to be confirmed, at appropriate intervals.

Activity 21 · 15 mins

S/NVQ D6

This Activity may provide the basis of appropriate evidence for your S/NVQ portfolio. If you are intending to take this course of action, it might be better to write your answers on separate sheets of paper.

In your own job, explain briefly how you:

■ explain work requirements to your team members in sufficient detail, and at a level and pace appropriate to each individual

_____

_____

_____

_____

■ confirm that the individuals concerned have a good understanding of work requirements, and are committed to meeting them

_____

_____

_____

_____

Now think about the effectiveness of your methods of communicating work requirements to the team, and try to find a way in which these methods could be improved. Explain what you intend to do that is different from your current approach.

_____

_____

_____

_____

_____

_____

_____

_____

_____

3.4 Setting performance standards

tne team

4 Set performance standards

5 Collect data to

We all know how difficult it is to judge whether something is successful when we don't have a clear standard against which to compare it.

To be meaningful, standards need to be expressed very clearly and should preferably be measurable.

Activity 22 . 4 mins

Think about your own workplace for a few minutes and then jot down **two** performance standards that are used there. Say whether each of them is measurable, and if so, what the unit of measure is.

_____

_____

_____

_____

Here are some suggestions of measurable standards, from a variety of industries.

Objective		Measure
'The level of impurities in the chemical produced should be less than 0.001%'	–	Quality or purity
'The average time to produce an airline reservation should be 2 minutes'	–	Process time
'The workplace should be accident free'	–	Accident rate
'Product costs should be less than budget'	–	Product costs
'Out-patients should not have to wait more than two hours'	–	Waiting time
'Response to emergency calls should not exceed 10 minutes'	–	Response time

In each of these cases a different measure is being applied.

Other types of measure may be used, such as error rate, scrap levels, quantities sold and so on.

In the real world, it is usually necessary to allow for some deviation from a defined standard. This 'acceptable deviation' is called a **tolerance**.

Here's an example of how tolerances are used. Suppose you have a bottle-filling plant that fills 500 ml (millilitre) bottles. You might have a tolerance of plus or minus 3 ml. That means that bottles holding quantities of 497 ml (500 − 3) to 503 ml (500 + 3) are acceptable. This tolerance is necessary to allow for the inevitable inaccuracies in the filling operation.

Unfortunately, it isn't possible in every single job to define measurable performance standards in this way. What do you do for instance if you are trying to measure 'willingness to help customers', 'attitude to the job' or 'ability to work under pressure'?

Often, a subjective comparison has to be made; in other words, the standard is inside somebody's head, and perhaps cannot be adequately defined in words, let alone numbers. So someone has to make a judgement – and one person's judgement of a particular performance or situation rarely coincides with another's.

| National Occupational Standards used in S/NVQs (Scottish and National Vocational Qualifications) are used in many organizations to help define performance standards for individuals. |

Wherever possible, then:

performance standards should be well defined and expressly stated.

Failing this, standards may be set by example. Some organizations demonstrate what good and bad customer service is, for instance, by showing videos of several examples of both.

The next two topics – collecting data and comparing results – are part of the monitoring process.

3.5 Collecting data

The collection of data is so routine in many workplaces that it tends to be taken for granted.

Each time you sign a time card, job sheet, materials requisition or shift log, you are putting your authority behind the accuracy of that information. No matter how humdrum and ordinary it seems, it is an indispensable part of a control process. Getting the job done depends on your carrying out procedures accurately and efficiently.

But there's more to it than that.

Activity 23

3 mins

In what other way do you collect data about what is happening in your work area? Jot down **one** way in which you collect data. (How do you keep up with what's going on?)

_____

_____

_____

_____

You may have thought of a number of ways of collecting data: talking to people or asking for reports for example. Every manager has his or her own approach to the job. One of the most common methods of keeping up with what is going on is also one of the best: we could best describe it as 'walking the job'.

The first line manager who goes round the work area several times a day and maintains a continuous contact with events builds up a great deal of useful information about the performance of the team.

By doing this, you can:

- give guidance based on your greater knowledge and experience;
- learn about problems and new ideas;
- find out how the team's plans are progressing;
- perhaps make minor adjustments and corrections to the plans so as to keep them on course.

This day-by-day, hour-by-hour interaction with the team is a normal and necessary part of supervision.

3.6 Comparing results with standards and objectives

The process of comparison should be quite straightforward, provided that:

- work objectives are well defined;
- performance standards are clear and precise;
- measurement of results is accurate.

Here are two examples.

> One standard for a high street bank is that no customer should be kept waiting in the queue for longer than five minutes. The average is three minutes. The bank feels confident that it is maintaining its own performance standards in this respect.

> In a food processing plant, the output target is 5000 cartons of biscuits per day. If the actual output is only 15,000 over a period of five days there is a major discrepancy – called a *variance* – between target and performance. It is a sign that the situation needs urgent attention.

But how often should performance be checked? Should the bank measure 'queue waiting time' in every branch on every day of the week – or is it good enough to take snap samples? Should the managers at the biscuit factory measure output every week – or every hour?

Activity 24

3 mins

Here are four situations where you might want to assess performance.

Decide what you think is the appropriate frequency for checking on performance or progress in each situation, and tick the appropriate box.

	Hourly	Daily	Weekly	Monthly	Annually
■ Which staff, and how many, are absent?	☐	☐	☐	☐	☐
■ Which machines are not working?	☐	☐	☐	☐	☐
■ What materials shortages do we have?	☐	☐	☐	☐	☐
■ What are our maintenance costs?	☐	☐	☐	☐	☐

Although there are no hard and fast rules to be applied, the two key points to be borne in mind are that:

■ everything you do takes up time, so you don't want to check anything unnecessarily frequently;

- you need to assess performance well before it becomes too late to take corrective action.

See whether the following answers would be appropriate in your job.

- **Which and how many staff are absent?**

Daily or weekly: it's unlikely that you would need to know from hour to hour, and checking monthly or annually would give you little chance to do much about high levels of absenteeism.

- **Which machines are not working?**

Hourly: presumably, urgent action needs to be taken to get a machine repaired and to reschedule work. Daily, weekly or monthly measurement may not be good enough, although in many situations a daily check may suffice.

- **What materials shortages do we have?**

Daily: once again, this would need to be followed up fairly swiftly, and daily measurement seems to be appropriate in most cases.

- **What are our maintenance costs?**

Monthly or annually: you would be more interested in this in the longer term – perhaps in comparing one year's performance against another.

However, there's plenty of room for disagreement about these answers. It depends largely on local circumstances. And you may have to alter your frequency of checking as a result of experience. The main point to remember is that:

the cost and effort of monitoring has to be balanced against the improvements in control that it can bring.

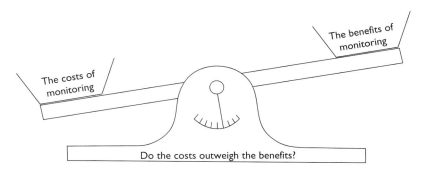

Comparing performance against standards too frequently involves unnecessary expense and work for no real return. Too infrequent comparisons can mean that danger signals are missed, which may result in losses in productivity and output.

3.7 Taking corrective action

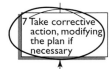

Now let's look at how we set about taking corrective action.

Activity 25 · 4 mins

Suppose you are in charge of production at a bakery and you have a work team of ten people. Your manager tells you that the productivity levels in your work area are not up to standard. You need to find the cause of the variance between what is expected and what is being achieved.

Jot down **three** possible lines of enquiry which you might investigate to see if you could find the cause of the variance.

_____

_____

_____

_____

_____

_____

Here are some of the things you might consider looking into.

- Is there faulty equipment?
- Is the equipment being properly used?
- How much absenteeism is there?
- Are you employing inexperienced work team members who aren't properly trained?
- Are wrong methods being used?
- Are materials up to standard?
- Are materials being used economically?

Once you have found the cause, you can put in place a suitable course of remedial action. If, for example, you decide that poor working practices are the cause of the variance, then staff training and increased supervision may help to improve things.

Of course, discovering the causes of an unfavourable variance and doing something about it is rarely as simple as just described. Nevertheless, when you're trying to solve a problem, it can help to bear in mind the following simple questions.

- Where are you now?
- Where do you want to get to?
- How can you get there?

But suppose in this case everything has been followed up – people, materials, machines, working methods and so on – and there still seems no way of improving productivity.

It may then be time to take a look at the situation in a wider context. It just might be that either the objectives or the standard are too demanding. In that case, it may be more sensible to change the standard rather than struggle to meet unreasonable targets.

What about the situation where you can see what is going wrong, think you know what to do about it, but are not in a position to take action? First line managers often have to seek authority to make changes, and must put forward recommendations to others.

Activity 26

S/NVQ D6

This Activity may provide the basis of appropriate evidence for your S/NVQ portfolio. If you are intending to take this course of action, it might be better to write your answers on separate sheets of paper.

If you have made recommendations in the past to more senior managers, to others at your level, to specialists, or perhaps to your team, how well did you do? Did you ensure that your recommendations:

- were based on sufficient, valid, and reliable information? ☐
- were consistent with team objectives, and with organizational values and policies? ☐
- took into account the impact of introducing change on other parts of the organization? ☐
- were made with minimum delay? ☐
- were presented in a clear and concise manner and form, consistent with organizational procedures? ☐

Assuming your recommendations, or the way you presented them, were less than perfect, what precisely will you do differently next time? Write down what you propose to change, and the way in which you will change it.

_____

_____

_____

_____

_____

_____

_____

_____

_____

_____

_____

_____

Self-assessment 2

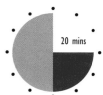

1   Fill in the missing words and arrows in the following diagram of a control loop.

2   Briefly explain why having clear objectives is a necessary part of good control.

_____

_____

_____

_____

_____

_____

_____

_____

3   There are **seven** statements listed below, each broken into two. Match each first half with the correct second half.

First halves	Second halves
All systems are controlled by setting a desired standard, and comparing results	against the improvements in control that it can bring.
Closed loop systems have feedback, monitoring and control,	against this standard.
Clear objectives are	well defined and expressly stated.
Performance standards should be	but open loop systems do not.
The big mistake is to assume that you don't need a plan,	necessary for good control.
The cost and effort of monitoring has to be balanced	because you think the what, why, who, how, when and where are all too self-evident.

4   The following sentences are examples of mission statements and objectives. Look at each one and decide what it is, then tick the appropriate box.

	Mission	Organizational	Project/ team	Task
a To produce a one-hour video on the problems of homelessness.	☐	☐	☐	☐
b Within the next three weeks to write the script for a one-hour video on the problems of homelessness which meets all the client's requirements and is within budget and delivered according to schedule.	☐	☐	☐	☐
c To provide free advice and assistance to homeless young people seeking accommodation in the Greater London area.	☐	☐	☐	☐
d To reduce the number of homeless young people living on the streets of London.	☐	☐	☐	☐

5 For each of the following incorrect statements, rewrite the part in italics, to make it correct.

    a Everything you do takes up your times, *so you shouldn't check anything*.

    _____

    _____

    b You need to assess performance after you've had enough time to study it – *in fact, as late as possible*.

    _____

    _____

    c Once a standard is set, it *is important not to allow any deviation from it*.

    _____

    _____

    d To be meaningful, standards need to be expressed very clearly and preferably *should be reversible*.

    _____

    _____

    e The best way to communicate with the team is to give *everyone the same information in the same way*.

    _____

    _____

    f Plans need to cover all the people within your area of responsibility, be realistic and achievable, and take account of *every person's needs and wants*.

    _____

    _____

    g A plan is *a rough and ready scheme for attaining an objective*.

    _____

    _____

    h The process of comparison should be quite straightforward, provided that work objectives are *known*, measurement of results is *possible* and performance standards are *roughly correct*.

    _____

    _____

Answers to these questions can be found on pages 114–15.

4 Summary

- **Closed loop** systems have feedback, monitoring and control. **Open loop** systems do not.

- All systems are controlled by setting a desired **standard**, and comparing results against this standard.

- The **stages** in controlling work are:

    - defining your objectives;
    - making a plan;
    - communicating with the team so that each team member knows the part he or she has to play;
    - setting performance standards;
    - collecting data to measure progress;
    - comparing results with standards and objectives;
    - taking corrective action.

- To achieve your plan, it is important that you know and can **define your objectives**. Having clear objectives is necessary for good control.

- Objectives can be **general** (organizational, project (or team) objectives) or **specific** (task objectives).

- **Specific objectives** must be SMART, that is **S**pecific, **M**easurable, **A**chievable, **R**elevant and **T**ime bound.

- It is important to **negotiate**, **agree** and **prioritize** specific task objectives with your team members.

- To make a plan, you need to answer the questions: **what? why? who? how? when?** and **where?**

- Communication is a **two-way process**, and implies information going in both directions: listening as well as talking.

- **Performance standards** should be well defined and expressly stated.

- The cost and effort of **monitoring** has to be balanced against the improvements in control that it can bring.

- When you're trying to **solve a problem**, it can help to bear in mind the following simple questions.

    - Where are you now?
    - Where do you want to get to?
    - How can you get there?

Session C
Planning and controlling the use of resources

1 Introduction

In this session, we will look at a number of resources: materials, plant and equipment and people. But we also consider other important topics. Quality is one of these; work flow and work methods are the others.

This session looks at the ways in which controlling resources contributes to planning and implementing a project. See also *Managing the Efficient Use of Materials* for more information on managing resources.

They are all important aspects of an organization's activities, they all require planning and controlling skills, and they all contribute to the realization of objectives.

Resources are essential, because they are the means by which objectives are achieved. **Quality** is vital, for it defines the standards to be reached. **Work flow** is important, as it can make the difference between a slipshod organization and an efficient one. **Work methods** are critical, in that they determine how well resources are used, and whether quality goals can be reached.

2 Controlling materials

In many workplaces, materials count for over 50 per cent of the total costs, so it's clearly important that control is kept over the way materials are looked after and used.

By 'materials', we mean anything needed for a work activity, such as building materials, or writing materials. Materials are not necessarily tangible – they may include information, for example.

Activity 27

3 mins

Using your own experience, jot down **three** problems that can arise in the use or care of materials, which may affect performance in your workplace.

_____

_____

_____

_____

Typical suggestions would include the following.

- Delays caused because materials are not available when and where they are needed.
- Raw materials wasted because the process in which they are being used has not been well thought out.
- Goods spoiled by rough handling or damage in transit.
- Too much time spent moving materials about rather than actually working with them.
- Information of the wrong type, or presented in a muddled manner.

Let's look at some of the major areas of responsibility for materials and see what kinds of control can be used. We'll think about:

- receiving;
- handling;
- processing;
- storing.

Whatever your job, you can probably fit your responsibilities for materials under these headings.

2.1 Receiving materials

We will start out considering those responsibilities for receiving materials.

Activity 28 · · 3 mins

You receive physical materials into your work area and you inspect them, or ask someone in your work team to do so, when they arrive.

Jot down **three** points about the delivery of materials which you would want to check.

_____

_____

_____

_____

_____

_____

_____

_____

_____

_____

_____

_____

You may have thought of a number of points, which could include the following.

■ Quantity

Have you received as much as you expected or ordered?

■ Condition

Are any of the goods damaged?

■ Destination

Where are the materials to be kept, or what are they to be used for in the immediate future in the workplace?

■ Specification

Are they what was ordered?

A simple form can provide a record of this information. Perhaps the organization where you work already has such a form. If not, you may be able to adapt the following one for your own purposes.

Departmental receiving report				
Dept.		Requisition No.	Date	
Checked by		Partial ☐　Complete ☐		
Qty	Description	Condition (state qty returned and reason)		Location

2.2 Handling materials

In your job, you may have to:

■ provide clear instructions (perhaps both in writing and verbally) on the safe use of equipment such as hand trucks, trolleys and so on;
■ draw up daily schedules for the use of handling equipment, so that materials can be moved in bulk where possible to save several trips to and from stores;
■ keep information secure;
■ keep a watchful eye on what is happening and make sure that materials are handled with care;
■ organize the work area so as to minimize unnecessary movement of materials.

Quite often, organizations issue specific instructions on the processes for major materials handling and the equipment to be used.

2.3 Processing materials

Processing materials refers to the use of materials in getting the job done – another prime area for control.

What is really needed is some kind of simple analysis that shows what materials were used at the start of the job, what the yield was and the amount of scrap, waste or rework which resulted.

Here is an excerpt from a **materials consumption variance report**, which gives this sort of information.

Materials consumption variance report			
Department: Art		Month: January 1997	
Material	Expected usage	Actual usage	Variance (%)
Paper, A2 size	550 sheets	655 sheets	+105 (+19.09%)
Paper, A3 size	1000 sheets	540 sheets	−460 (−46%)
Paint, cobalt blue	250 tubs	180 tubs	−70 (−28%)
Paint, crimson	250 tubs	280 tubs	+30 (+12%)

This form shows standards, actual results and variances for materials consumption – three or four stages of control.

The variance is worked out by subtracting the actual amount used from the standard – in this case, the expected consumption. It is shown first as the actual number of items and then as a percentage variance from the standard.

The variance report gives the manager an opportunity to identify major variances, so that corrective action can be taken.

2.4 Storing materials

It's quite likely that materials spend quite a bit of time in your work area, rather than in the safety of a central warehouse, and that you are responsible for them while they are there.

Activity 29 · 3 mins

Jot down **three** responsibilities you have, as a result of materials and goods being in your work area.

_____

_____

_____

_____

_____

_____

Typical responsibilities might include the following.

- Checking stock levels in the work area and making sure there is enough of each item to meet anticipated demand.
- Being responsible for safe storage. This might include knowing about proper floor loads, stacking heights, shelf strengths and special precautions for storing fragile and flammable materials. For the safe storage of information, you may have to think about protecting and backing up data.
- Making sure goods are safe from theft. Even if the goods are not valuable in themselves, you may have to be aware of security, including that of information, such as personal data records.
- Making sure materials are protected from damage. For example: some items may need protection from heat or cold; others may have to be completely enclosed.

Once again, to maintain control effectively you need to set standards. Let's look at an example.

Activity 30 · 4 mins

Here are some details about the use of materials in a certain work area.

Normally, 800 units a day are used, and ten days' supply is ordered at one time. At peak times (three months of the year) the demand increases by 50 per cent, so the order level has to go up proportionately.

Once the order for materials is sent out, it takes three days for them to be delivered. In addition, an extra three days' supply is normally held, to protect against delays or sudden, unforeseen demand; this is called the safety stock.

If you were the manager, at what level of stock would you place a new order, and what maximum stock levels would you expect?

_____

_____

_____

_____

_____

Perhaps you agree that, when six days' requirements are left, you would need to place a new order. This is because you want to keep three days' supply as safety stock and you have to allow another three days for delivery. During most of the year the re-order level will be:

$6 \times 800 = 4{,}800$ units (of which the safety stock is $3 \times 800 = 2{,}400$ units).

At peak times, this will go up by 50 per cent, that is, the re-order level will be:

$6 \times 1{,}200 = 7{,}200$ units (of which the safety stock is $3 \times 1{,}200 = 3{,}600$ units).

The maximum stock level will occur when a new delivery has just arrived, and the safety stock is still in the store, that is:

$$2{,}400 + 8{,}000 = 10{,}400 \text{ units, at normal times}$$

$$3{,}600 + 12{,}000 = 15{,}600 \text{ units, at peak times}$$

Here is that information summarized as diagrams.

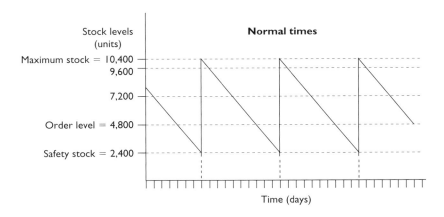

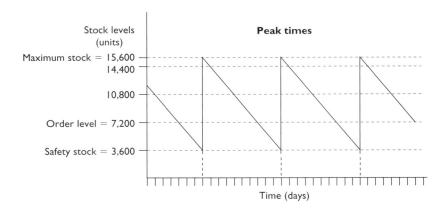

Calculations like these will enable you to work out when to order more supplies, and will provide a guide to when to follow up and check stock levels.

If responsibility for materials is part of your job, you may well also be expected
to make good estimates of:

■ usage;
■ time required to replenish goods;
■ likely delays;
■ likely changes in demand caused by overtime, rush orders or seasonal
variation.

2.5 Materials control and computers

Computers can store large amounts of data and provide access to information very quickly. Thus the entire materials holding of an organization can be
recorded in a central computer **database**. Terminals situated throughout
the plant and offices can allow immediate access to designated blocks of data
to authorized personnel.

It is possible to organize a completely automatic re-ordering system, so that –
in theory at least – stocks are always at the correct level. However, computers
are only as accurate as the information input into them. It is therefore important to have adequate controls over input data.

If you use computers in your job, you will no doubt be aware that computers
are only another tool of management. It is preferable for these roles not to
be reversed!

3 Controlling quality

Whatever your job, the quality of products you make or the services you provide will be judged by your customer. (Don't forget that a customer can be internal to the organization as well as external.)

Quality isn't only about **finish**, or **features**, or **price**, or **delivery**, or **presentation**.

Quality involves all the characteristics of a product or service.

A recipe for quality contains certain key ingredients. They are listed in the CASCADE formula.

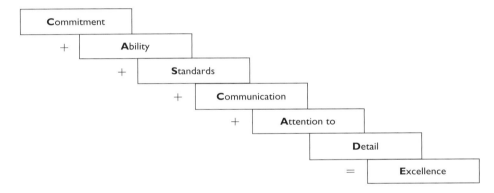

We've already discussed standards, and we'll do so again shortly. But high quality can't be achieved **simply** through setting standards. Let's turn our attention for a moment therefore to the other points listed in this 'recipe'.

Activity 31

3 mins

Jot down in your own words what you understand by the phrase 'a commitment to quality'.

_____

_____

_____

_____

_____

_____

Compare your response with the following.

Commitment to quality means the dedication and determination that people need in order to bring quality of work to a high standard and to keep it there.

When a manager is fully committed to quality it is usually plain for everyone to see. It will be obvious to the customers, because they will be able to rely on receiving consistently high quality. It will also be obvious to the work team, and they will tend to become fully committed themselves.

Ability to achieve quality refers to know-how and training, which enable quality goals to be translated into quality work. Team members can't be expected to meet quality standards if they are untrained or unskilled in the work.

Communication is the link between those who set the standards and those who have to interpret them, and between those who do the work and those who measure the results. As we've already discussed, communication is a two-way affair.

Good communication is arguably the most important factor in the success of any work team. If the team leader has a good understanding with the team, and if the team members freely exchange ideas and problems, half the battle is won.

Good communication results in good understanding.

Attention to detail marks the difference between having good intentions about quality and actually achieving results.

Getting the quality right is hard work.

Maintaining quality is something that has to be worked at on a daily basis. It can't just be left to look after itself.

You need to get your team to 'think quality'. The following tips may help.

- When you see some work that you feel could have been done better, or are doubtful about, try asking the question 'Are **you** happy with this?' rather than criticizing the work. Or ask the team to judge. You may find that the team's standards are higher than your own.
- Encourage discussions about quality and standards of workmanship.
- Keep the team informed. Let them know how their work is received by the people most directly affected by their work – their customers. Let them know how their contribution fits into the whole scheme of things.
- Put quality records on display, where everyone can see them.

■ Be generous with your praise when you see someone make a special effort, or achieve a significant result. Resist the temptation to moan when things don't go so well.

■ Lead by example: show that you care about quality.

3.1 Quality and standards

If quality is to be adequately controlled, it should be measurable against standards.

The standard for a particular commodity or service must be written down in such a way that it is clear exactly what criteria the product must meet. This is necessary so that any differences between the standard and the product can be assessed, and, if necessary, corrected.

To take two examples as follows.

> A company producing a technical item such as a radio or television will have specifications for each individual component, indicating the size, value and other characteristics. If the components are delivered in batches, sample items can be measured, in order that the likelihood of the batch conforming to the specification can be determined. Then, when the components are made up into subassemblies, their perform- ance is also measured. Finally, the end product is tested, to make sure it complies with the product specification.

> Organizations delivering something that is not measurable, such as a financial service, may use independent assessors to evaluate the per- formance of their products. For small companies, this 'comparison with a standard' may be carried out by one individual. The quality standards of a small hairdressing business, for instance, may be set and continuously assessed by the owner. Larger organizations, such as store chains, typically control standards of service partly through staff training programmes, and partly by carefully monitoring the response of its customers.

The most important thing is for an organization to have a well-defined **quality system** that can ensure products meet an agreed standard of quality **consist- ently**. In other words, checking or sampling products for quality is essential, but an even more important requirement is a system that ensures that products are made or supplied to the right level of quality in the first place.

The quality of a product or service is a reflection of the way the producer or supplier is organized and managed.

A quality system can be defined as:

> 'the organizational structure, responsibilities, procedures, processes, and resources, for implementing quality management.'
>
> Dennis F. Kehoe, *The Fundamentals of Quality Management*[2]

The British Standards Institution, working with international bodies such as the International Organization for Standardization (ISO), has developed the quality systems standard **BS EN ISO 9000**, which has been updated and is now known as ISO 9000:2000.

ISO 9000:2000 sets out a number of steps or elements that define what organizations have to do to set up and maintain an adequate quality system. If they do this to the satisfaction of the awarding body, they are given accreditation to the standard.

What's in this standard? To give a flavour of what it contains, we'll go over a few major points. ISO 9000 encompasses the following areas.

■ **The quality system**

The system must be fully documented, the principal document being the **Quality Manual**, which sets out all the procedures for implementing the system.

■ **Management responsibility**

Every organization is required to have a documented **quality policy**, which must be read and understood by all employees, together with an organization chart showing who is responsible for what. A key appointment is a management representative. This person ensures that all aspects of the standard are complied with, and reports to the organization's senior management on the performance of the quality system.

■ **Resources, procedures and processes**

All the resources of the organization should be managed in such a way that they support the objective of quality. This means human resources, the environment in which they work and the tools and equipment they use to do their jobs.

Where appropriate, procedures relating to production, customer relationships, product design, materials procurement, and inventory management should be established with the aims of quality and customer satisfaction in mind. This requirement only needs to be met so far as it is relevant to the organization. For instance, a firm of solicitors is unlikely to need an elaborate inventory management system.

[2] Published by Chapman and Hall, 1996.

All the processes in the organization should be capable of measurement, not only to ensure that quality standards are being met but to identify ways of improving in the future. The requirements are explained in much more detail in *Providing Quality to Customers.*

■ **Purchasing**

The suppliers to an organization should either have ISO 9000 accreditation themselves, or the organization must assess their quality assurance system.

■ **Product identification and traceability**

Purchased goods and services must always be traceable to the company that supplies the product. The organization's manufactured products must be traceable to suppliers of the raw materials, production batches, and, if appropriate, to specific operators, shifts or machines. In addition, all parts have to be clearly identified.

■ **Process control**

Work processes must be documented and controlled to prevent error, and to ensure the customer's exact requirements are met. Clear work instructions, training, planning, and equipment must all be provided. In addition, the various stages of production must be documented, so that product faults can be identified and rectified quickly.

■ **Inspection and testing**

Inspection and testing operations for incoming goods, in-process work, and for the final product, have to be documented and the performance of them controlled.

■ **Corrective and preventative action**

Whenever a product fault occurs, or a supplier does not deliver goods or services as agreed, or customers complain, or there are internal problems within the organization, the cause must be identified, and steps taken to prevent any recurrence.

■ **Internal quality audits**

The organization must carry out internal quality audits, to ensure the quality system is working satisfactorily.

At this point, it would be tempting to say 'so much for quality', as if this brief section had said all there was to say on the subject. In fact, we have hardly skimmed the surface, and you might consider whether you should study this important discipline further. There are related titles in this series listed at the back of this workbook, such as *Providing Quality to Customers.*

4 Controlling plant and equipment

The responsibility first line managers have for plant and equipment varies a great deal. Almost certainly, you will have responsibility for the way some of the equipment in your area is used from day to day.

Let's look at two typical critical control points that will concern many first line managers.

- Providing adequate working space and arranging equipment in the workplace.
- Maintaining and servicing equipment.

4.1 Assessing space and arranging equipment

If you are serious about making the best use of the space available, it's probably a good idea to draw up some kind of floor-plan of the work area which shows:

- the layout of the walls, doors and windows, drawn to scale;
- the location of equipment that cannot be moved;
- access to services, such as water and electricity;
- routes people and materials tend to take.

There are a number of software packages available to help you do this. The diagram below is an example.

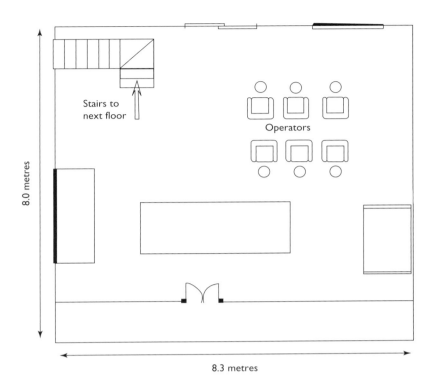

Activity 32

4 mins

Suppose you are going to lay out a new work area for your work team. (If you don't have a fixed work area, imagine you are laying out a new office or shop floor.)

Jot down **three** things that you would try to achieve in your layout. Here's one suggestion to get you started.

■ Accessibility – so that it is easy to get to any part of the work area.

_____

_____

_____

_____

Here are some other points that you may have included in your list.

■ Maximum flexibility

Can the layout be changed reasonably quickly to meet changing circumstances, perhaps for meetings or training?

■ **Best use of volume**

Are you using all the space (up to the ceiling?) as effectively as possible? This is particularly important in storage areas.

■ **Maximum visibility**

Can you see the whole work area at once? Are there any unplanned out-of-sight areas?

■ **Minimum distance**

How much do people have to move about unnecessarily? Are routes direct?

■ **Minimum handling**

This follows from the previous point. Moving things about can be tiring, and risks damaging them.

■ **Minimum discomfort**

Is the area draught-free so far as possible? Is the lighting adequate? Are the heating and air-conditioning levels appropriate?

■ **Maximum safety**

Are there any avoidable or unidentified hazards? For example, is there adequate space around machines? Are safety controls such as emergency alarms within reach? Are emergency exits accessible?

■ **Security**

Are expensive items kept in well-lit areas in full view, preferably under lock and key? Is access limited to those who need to enter the area?

■ **One-way flow**

If practicable, work should flow in one direction through the area so as to avoid cross traffic.

To assess how well workspace is used, various measures can be used. One is to talk in terms of 'output per square metre'.

Activity 33 · 3 mins

Can you think of another way to measure how well space is used?

_____

_____

_____

_____

There are several possibilities, including:

- square metre per employee – useful for planning for people's needs during a period of expansion;
- productive area as a proportion of the total floor space, in square metres – an overall measure of how much space is used for the actual job;
- unused space as a proportion of the total floor space – a measure of non-productive space;
- used space as a proportion of total volume – useful for designated storage areas.

When you are changing things around, you may need to assess your proposed new layout in these kinds of terms.

4.2 Maintaining plant and equipment

Perhaps your workplace, like many others, has a separate maintenance department. Nevertheless, maintenance is normally part of the responsibility of every first line manager.

You probably have responsibility for:

- getting a normal life's work out of the equipment in your area;
- reporting failures as soon as they happen;
- arranging for regular maintenance;
- training the work team in good habits, so that equipment is not misused.

There are two aspects of maintenance:

- breakdown maintenance – getting a machine repaired when it fails;
- preventative maintenance – carrying out routine inspections and parts replacement to prevent failure.

Activity 34

3 mins

If you were responsible for operating a preventative maintenance system for some equipment under your control, what information do you think you would need? Write down **one** item of information that you would feel to be necessary.

_____

_____

_____

_____

You could have answered:

■ how frequently each item of equipment should be serviced;
■ exactly what has to be done during each service.

Some useful documents would be the following.

■ **A maintenance schedule**

This lists all equipment and states when and how it should be serviced. The information is based on the manufacturer's recommendation and on past experience. There may also be a statutory requirement for regular, scheduled checks, for example on pressure vessels and relief valves.

■ **Checklists**

A checklist is like a guided tour of the equipment. It describes the important points of a machine, in a systematic sequence. It provides instructions on how to spot trouble or possible failures, and gives information as to what to do about them.

The following is an example of a checklist.

Component or system	Instructions	Monthly	Quarterly	Six monthly
Electrical	Inspect switch for poor contact or short. Replace if necessary.	X		
	Look at wire for fraying or loose connections. Replace if necessary.	X		
Table	Test table settings for tightness. Adjust if necessary.		X	

Preparing lists of inspection and maintenance instructions is obviously a task that requires considerable knowledge and experience, as well as time and attention. However, such lists are effective tools in the control of equipment.

5 Controlling work methods

In all probability, you frequently have to make decisions about:

- what is to be done;
- who is to do it;
- how it is to be done.

In every decision you make you are defining standards.

Activity 35

5 mins

Think of any job at work that you might ask one of your work team to do.

Jot down some of the information you would include regarding the standard for the job. Try to think of at least **four** items.

_____

_____

_____

_____

_____

_____

Assuming that your work team aren't experts in the job you are asking them to do, they would need several pieces of information.

Listed below are the main headings. See whether you can fit the points you've suggested under these headings.

- Method

  This may need to be a clear, unambiguous statement of the steps to be taken.

- Equipment

  This is especially important if there is a choice to be made.

■ **Time**

You may have to specify how long the job should take. You may have derived a standard time using work study methods, or you may just have to use your judgement as to what is a reasonable time to complete the work.

■ **Materials**

This may be a list of ingredients or a drawing.

■ **Production aids**

Any fixtures, utensils, small tools, software, workstations, or other devices needed to carry out the job may have to be listed.

■ **Quantity**

A clear indication should be given of the amount of work to be done, including the quantity of materials to be used.

The list will vary according to the experience and seniority of the team members involved.

The amount of detail provided will depend largely on the experience of the people doing the job.

Here is one example of a work method definition.

Title: Vegetable Risotto

Materials and **quantities** required:

1 small onion	pinch of mixed herbs
1 stick celery	salt and pepper
1 tomato	½ teaspoon (2.5 ml) yeast extract
2 oz. (50 g) mushrooms	2 teaspoons (10 ml) tomato purée
2 oz. (50 g) raw rice	1 oz. (25 g) cheddar cheese, grated
8 fl oz. (225 ml) vegetable stock	

Cooking **method**

1 Chop the onion, celery, tomato and mushrooms and put into a small pan (**equipment**) with the vegetable stock, herbs and rice.

2 Bring to the boil over a gas ring or hot-plate (**production aids**), cover and simmer for about 20 minutes (**time**) until the rice is tender and the stock absorbed.

3 Add seasoning and yeast extract to taste, and stir in the tomato puree.

4 Serve with grated cheese.

Most people could probably manage to produce a meal of an acceptable standard by following the work method above.

Notice that there is some scope in this method, to allow for personal taste, in the amount of seasoning that is added. That may make the difference between a delicious meal and a disaster!

The more precisely performance standards of this kind are defined, the greater the control.

Next, we turn from the control of work methods to the control of work flow.

6 Scheduling work flow

Control of the flow of work is often a critical consideration for any first line manager. You may be expected to achieve a defined amount of work in a fixed period, and have responsibility for meeting that target by employing your work team and equipment effectively.

Let's look at an example of a work flow problem.

Activity 36 · 4 mins

Imagine you are in charge of three separate work centres or work teams and you are asked to complete four orders in the coming week. Each order will go to all three of the work centres, but they will go to them in different sequences, and for different lengths of time.

Here is a chart showing you what is required from each order and in what sequence, assuming one working day equals eight hours. To take an example, the requirement for order number 3 is that work centre B should perform operation 1 (six hours), work centre A performs operation 2 (four hours), and work centre C performs operation 3 (eight hours).

Order no.	1			2			3			4		
Operation sequence	1	2	3	1	2	3	1	2	3	1	2	3
Work centre	A	B	C	C	A	B	B	A	C	A	C	B
Estimated time (hrs)	4	8	2	10	4	6	6	4	8	4	10	12

Describe briefly how you would set about scheduling these operations.

_____

_____

_____

_____

_____

_____

Perhaps you said you would draw up a plan, schedule or timetable showing the orders planned for each work centre each day.

One type of chart useful in this situation is called a **Gantt chart**, named after the American industrial engineer Henry Laurence Gantt who developed it around 1915.

Here's what one version of our figure might look like when drawn in on a Gantt chart.

Work centre		Gant chart						
		(O = Order number, and idle periods are shaded)						
A	O1				O2		O3	
B		O1				O2	O3	
C			O1	O2				O3
Day	Monday	Tuesday	Wednesday	Thursday	Friday	Monday	Tuesday

Activity 37

3 mins

Look at the chart above and jot down **two** problems that would arise from organizing the flow of work in the way this chart shows.

_____

_____

The flow of work is orderly and systematic, but you probably realized that:

- only three orders are completed;
- even the three orders that are completed aren't finished within a week as required: they go into Tuesday of the following week;
- equipment is going to be standing idle for long periods of time.

This version does not achieve what we want, so we must try again. It's largely a matter of trial and error.

Activity 38

15 mins

Experiment with the blank chart below and try to arrange the work so that it is completed by the end of the week, and keeps to the required operation and work centre sequence for each order. (Hint: you will need to re-arrange the orders.) Two copies of the blank chart are given, in case you don't succeed on your first attempt.

Order no.	1			2			3			4		
Operation sequence	1	2	3	1	2	3	1	2	3	1	2	3
Work centre	A	B	C	C	A	B	B	A	C	A	C	B
Estimated time (hrs)	4	8	2	10	4	6	6	4	8	4	10	12

Gantt chart						
Work centre						
A						
B						
C						
Day	Monday	Tuesday	Wednesday	Thursday	Friday	Monday

Gantt chart						
Work centre						
A						
B						
C						
Day	Monday	Tuesday	Wednesday	Thursday	Friday	Monday

Here are two possible solutions. You may well have thought of a different version.

Gantt chart					
Work center	(O = Order number, and idle periods are shaded)				
A	O1 O4 [idle] O2		[idle]	O3	[idle]
B	[idle] O1	[idle]	O2 O3	O4	[idle]
C	O2	[idle] O1	O4	[idle]	O3
Day	Monday	Tuesday	Wednesday	Thursday	Friday

Gantt chart					
Work centre	(O = Order number, and idle periods are shaded)				
A	O4 O1 O3			O2	
B	O3	O1	O4	O2	
C	O4	O2	O3	O1	
Day	Monday	Tuesday	Wednesday	Thursday	Friday

You can see that, by re-arranging the orders, it is possible to complete them all within five days. There is no magic formula for devising work schedules – it's often largely a matter of trial and error. The process can be time-consuming, but saving half a day in your work schedule more than compensates for having to spend half an hour on the Gantt chart. Also, there are software packages that will do the job faster.

The Gantt chart provides a clear picture of:

- what needs to be achieved at every work centre each day;
- when the work centres are idle.

The techniques we have discussed are useful and, with some modifications, can be applied to many kinds of work. In the next session, we'll look at the use of a Gantt chart in planning a project that is composed of a number of jobs.

Drawing up plans and schedules like these can be quite a challenging task. Persuading the work team to follow them is another challenge.

Self-assessment 3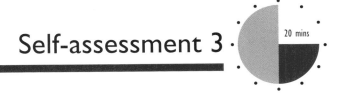

20 mins

1   Here are some problems associated with the control of materials, and a list of possible solutions. Match each problem with the most appropriate solution.

	Problem		Possible solution
a	A delay is caused because materials are not available when and where they are needed.	i	Improve handling methods.
b	Materials are wastefully used.	ii	Ensure that materials are ordered in sufficient quantities, and to the correct specification.
c	Materials are found to be damaged when they are about to be used.	iii	Monitor the consumption rate of each type of material more carefully.
d	Materials are found to be of the wrong type, just when they are about to be used.	iv	Increase security in the stores area.
e	Too much of one kind of material is in stock, and too little of another kind.	v	Improve ordering and goods receiving procedures.
f	Pilfering of materials occurs.	vi	Improve work methods to make more efficient use of materials.

2 The following are taken from our discussions on quality. Match each heading or name in the left column with its correct description, taken from the column on the right.

a Documented quality policy	i The dedication and determination that people need in order to bring quality of work to a high standard and to keep it there.
b Quality manual	ii Know-how and training, which enable quality goals to be translated into quality work.
c Quality	iii All the characteristics of a product or service.
d Quality system	iv The difference between having good intentions about quality and actually achieving results.
e Ability to achieve quality	v The link between those who set the standards and those who have to interpret them, and between those who do the work and those who measure the results.
f Commitment to quality	vi Ensures that products are made or delivered to the right level of quality in the first place.
g Communication	vii Must be read and understood by all employees, and contains an organization chart showing who is responsible for what.
h Attention to detail	viii Sets out all the procedures for implementing the system.

7 Summary

- Four major areas of **responsibility** when controlling materials are:

  - receiving;
  - handling;
  - processing;
  - storage.

- A recipe for quality is the **cascade formula**: Commitment plus Ability plus Standards plus Communication plus Attention to Detail – result Excellence.

- The **quality** of a product or service is a reflection of the way the producer or supplier is organized and managed.

- **ISO 9000:2000** sets out a number of steps or elements that define what organizations have to do to set up and maintain an adequate quality system. If they do this to the satisfaction of the awarding body, they are given **accreditation** to the standard.

- **Standards** used in **controlling work methods** may be based on: the method to be employed, the equipment to be used, the time to be taken, which materials are to be used, production aids, the quantities to be used.

- First line managers have responsibilities for making sure that equipment under their control is properly **maintained**.

- **Gantt charts** are useful devices when planning work schedules.

Session D
Planning and controlling projects

1 Introduction

'He had been eight years upon a project for extracting sun-beams out of cucumbers, which were to be put into vials hermetically sealed, and let out to warm the air in raw inclement summers.' – Jonathan Swift, *Gulliver's Travels* (1726)

We have all planned and controlled projects of one sort or another. You may have undertaken projects in your job: setting up a new work area, for example, or conducting a customer survey. Outside of work, most of us have taken on home projects, such as decorating a room, embroidering a tapestry, or building a wall.

Projects are activities with specific aims, and usually last for a limited length of time. We know when a project has started, and when it has finished. It is interesting and useful to consider the approaches and techniques used in projects, for they are applicable in many areas of work.

We start by discussing what projects are, and what project managers do. Then we go on to look at project planning and project costs.

2 Project management

A project is an undertaking of work that has a definite beginning and a definite end. Typically, resources – people, materials, workspace and so on – are assigned for a limited period in order to achieve defined objectives.

The planning and controlling of projects is called project management. A project manager has the task of identifying resources, and organizing them effectively and efficiently.

Activity 39 · 3 mins

From the information on the previous page, try to identify **two** ways in which project management differs from most other kinds of management.

_____

_____

_____

_____

_____

_____

A project manager, unlike most other managers, has to:

- work to definite ends, and within a specified time period;
- control resources on a temporary basis, after which many of them will be released for other activities or uses.

EXTENSION 3
If you'd like to read more about project management, the books listed on pages 112–13 are worth reading.

So project management is in some ways easier: you know that the task will finish once you have achieved your objectives, and that you and your team can focus on these objectives without being distracted by unrelated tasks.

However, project managers often have to work to very tight constraints, and may therefore find themselves under stress because of this. Also, some or all of the project team may be working on more than one project at the same time.

Project constraints are related to:

- **costs**, which determine the amount of resources available;
- **time**, which is seldom in sufficient supply;
- **quality**, which involves all the characteristics of the project outcome.

It is important to remember that the stages of project control are no different from any other kind of work control; the diagram we saw earlier is still applicable.

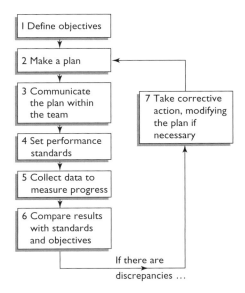

3 The germ of a project

How do projects come about? Normally, someone – a customer, or the organization's senior management – will define a broad objective. Every project:

- begins its life as an idea, conceived in somebody's head;
- is usually proposed either as a solution to a problem, or as a means of exploiting an opportunity.

Projects can be large or small.

Activity 40

Think of **one** or **two** projects you have been involved in, and try to summarize the idea(s) the original project proposer must have had.

_____

_____

_____

_____

_____

_____

Some examples of project proposals are as follows.

- The marketing staff of a company making washing powder proposes that an existing product be modified to make it more environmentally friendly, which their surveys tell them customers want.
- A catering manager decides it's time to design a new menu.
- The overworked partners in a legal practice decide they would like to recruit two more clerks, to take over some of the routine tasks.
- A first line manager decides to reorganize her team's work area.
- The senior managers of an organization that is expanding decide that a new location must be found to house some of its activities.
- The safety officer of an organization proposes to set up training courses for all managers, to ensure they are acquainted with new health and safety legislation.
- A team leader wants to get his team to be more aware of customers' needs.
- A nursing supervisor is asked to devise an improved booking-in system for patients.
- A manager decides she would like to reorganize the department's paperwork system, to cut down on bureaucracy.
- A customer of a training company requests a new course designed for its specific needs.
- A finance manager, dissatisfied with the organization's accounting system, proposes that its computers should be upgraded.

At the earliest stage, proposers cannot be sure that the project will be realizable, within time, cost and quality constraints. They therefore need answers to the questions: 'Can we afford it? Can it be done in the required timescale? Will it meet all our needs?'

For a large project, it will not normally be possible to determine the answers to these questions without further detailed analysis. A **feasibility study** may therefore be set up. Such a study will look into all aspects of the proposal, by making costs calculations, identifying possible problems, and attempting to predict what will happen if the project goes ahead.

A feasibility study isn't usually necessary for smaller projects; instead, the feasibility aspects are considered as part of the project planning. In either case, the more thought and analysis that takes place during the early stages, the more successful the project is likely to be.

4 Knowing what you want to achieve

Suppose you are assigned as leader of a project, and have a team to work with you. How do you begin?

Activity 41

4 mins

What do you think should be the first few activities for any project, before the planning stage?

_____

_____

_____

_____

_____

_____

_____

_____

_____

Even if a feasibility study has already taken place, the team will need to do the following.

- Discuss the project at some length: *'What's it all about?'*
- Get together all the information they can collect about the subject of the project: *'How can we acquire knowledge?'*
- Make sure the objectives are very clearly understood, distinguishing between those that are essential and those that are only desirable: *'What must we achieve?'*
- Perhaps look at similar earlier projects: the way that other teams have gone about things, and the lessons they learned: *'Has this been done before? When and how?'*
- Know what the constraints are, in terms of costs, quality and time: *'What are the controls and restrictions on our work?'*
- Identify how individual team members' knowledge and experience can contribute to the approach: *'What do we know? What can we do?'*

You may find that lack of time or resources makes it impossible for you to achieve all the specific objectives given to you. In this situation you must prioritize the objectives by assessing their **importance** and **urgency**, and then putting them in the order in which they will be done.

Activity 42

5 mins

1   Make a list of the tasks facing you during the next few days.
    For each one, ask yourself the following questions.

    ■ How important is it?
    ■ How urgently must it be carried out?

2   Write each task down in the appropriate box on the chart below.

3   Number the tasks in each box in order of priority.

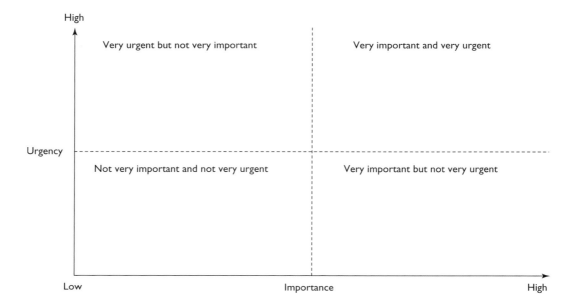

By using this guide, you can prioritize your tasks, starting with the very important and very urgent ones, and gradually working your way down the list until
you reach the least important and least urgent.

During these initial activities, the team will have the opportunity to get to
know one another better.

The next step is to make a plan.

5 Project planning

You will remember the list we looked at earlier, which said that the plan should consider:

'Amid a multitude of projects, no plan is devised.' – Publius Syrus, *Moral Sayings* (1st century BC)

- **what**, exactly, is to be done;
- **why** the work is being done: for whose benefit;
- **who** is to do each part of the work;
- **how** it is to be done: the approach, processes and techniques to be used;
- **when** the work is to be started and completed, and perhaps dates for agreed 'milestones' while the project is in progress;
- **where** it is to be done.

5.1 Deciding what is to be done

You learned in Session A, **3.1 Defining objectives** that, before carrying out any task, you must break it down into specific objectives that define the tasks that you are trying to achieve. These objectives must be SMART, that is they must be **S**pecific, **M**easurable, **A**chievable, **R**elevant and **T**ime bound.

5.2 Identifying why the work needs to be done

A key question to consider when defining objectives of any kind is 'Why are we doing this', in other words 'Who are we doing it for?' All work is for somebody's benefit, and that somebody is usually a customer.

Everyone has customers. If you serve in a shop, your customers are the people who come in to buy goods and services. If you work in the storeroom behind the shop, your direct customers are probably fellow members of staff who depend on the service you provide. Some employees have to think about more than one group of customers. For example, a zoo-keeper must be concerned about both the welfare of the animals and the interest of the visitors.

So you need to be clear about both what you are aiming to achieve and why you are doing it, in other words who the customer is and what they want from you. This information will be extremely helpful in enabling you to complete the objective successfully.

5.3 Deciding who will do what

Few teams are composed of an ideal selection of members. If you, as project leader, have any say in the matter, you will obviously want people on your team with a range of skills, all relevant to the demands of the project. However, even if each individual is an expert in his or her own sphere of activity, it does not mean to say that the group, once gathered as a team, will combine well.

So, you will need to act, first and foremost, as a team leader. You will need to demonstrate that you:

- are committed to the project and to the team;
- will support them, and do everything you can to make them, and the project, a success;
- are looking for their support;
- believe every team member has an important part to play.

You will need to recognize, too, that teams, once they have been formed, tend to go through a **storming** phase. There is bound to be some uncertainty, as people 'find their feet', and this can lead to conflict. Individuals are trying to discover the answers to the following questions.

- 'Where do I fit in?'
- 'What will the others expect of me?'
- 'What can I expect from them?'
- 'How difficult will this task be?'
- 'What resources do I need, and how will I tackle this job?'
- 'What kind of leader have we got here?'

This storming phase may show itself as open disagreement, by the group splitting into factions, or perhaps simply as a general air of nervousness.

Activity 43 · 3 mins

List **three** steps you think you could take, as team leader, to help the team through this storming phase.

_____

_____

_____

_____

_____

As leader, you will need to take the initiative, by:

- showing that you are confident of success, and have clear ideas about how to achieve it;
- encouraging open discussion of all relevant issues;
- focusing on the task in hand, rather than on personalities;
- summarizing the arguments once discussion has taken place and, if possible, getting a general agreement;
- avoiding situations in which one viewpoint wins and another loses, and giving credit for all good ideas;
- giving the team time to settle down.

If you want to study team building, and the phases that teams go through, in more detail, you may like to study *Building the Team* in this series. See the list at the back of this workbook.

When assigning tasks, it is worth remembering that work should ideally challenge an individual, without being so demanding that the person is unable to cope. Tasks that are too easy may result in boredom and dissatisfaction; tasks that are too difficult may lead to failure and loss of confidence.

The team leader, of course, has plenty of challenges, and this is not the least of them.

5.4 Planning how the work will be done

What is the best way to tackle the project? What resources will the team need? Which techniques should be applied? What processes should be used?

For a sizeable project, these questions can seem to be very daunting. Like any task that threatens to overwhelm, it's best to break a large project into smaller components. There are a number of advantages to this approach.

- If you have a team of people, each with skills and experience in particular aspects of the work, they should be able to help you identify separate jobs, and suggest suitable methods of accomplishing them.
- Each person may be able to take responsibility for some of the jobs.
- It may be possible to identify and assign separate resources for each part of the work.
- Often, some of the jobs can proceed independently of the others.
- You will usually be able to identify milestones (as we will discuss shortly), which will help you keep the project to time.
- It will be easier to keep track of finances, as each job can be costed separately.

5.5 Planning the 'when'

You will recall that we used a version of the Gantt chart for scheduling work flow in Session C. The chart is also useful for planning project timescales. Look at this illustration.

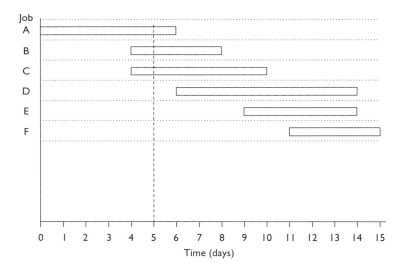

This looks rather different from the earlier Gantt chart, but it is essentially the same. Its base is measured in time, as before, and this time the vertical scale is marked off in 'jobs', rather than 'work centres'.

In this example project, six separate jobs have been identified. Each job is represented as a horizontal bar or rectangle, the length of which is an estimate of the time for the job. The vertical dotted line is the review date.

The thick horizontal lines underneath the bars show the progress made up to that date; the length of these lines indicate the actual amount of time spent on each job. As an example, four days have been spent on Job A, out of the five scheduled.

This is only one of several possible ways that Gantt charts may be used for planning project timescales.

Another, more useful planning system, is the **critical path method (CPM)**. This provides more information, but takes more effort in its preparation.

First, the jobs to be completed are listed in a table, as illustrated in the example below.

Project: Install machine at new site				
Job	Activity	Estimated time (days)	Precede by	Follow by
A	Planning stage	5	–	BDG
B	Clear site	2	A	C
C	Dig foundation	4	B	E
D	Take delivery of machine	I	A	I
E	Lay concrete	3	C	F
F	Install machine	3	E	I
G	Run services to site	4	A	H
H	Connect services	2	G	I
I	Testing stage	5	DFH	–

The time to complete each job is entered (shown here in the third column), and the jobs that must precede and follow each job are shown (in columns 4 and 5). For example, before the foundation can be dug (Job C), the site must be cleared (Job B). Once this has been done, the concrete can be laid (Job E). The only job that must be completed before any work can start is the planning stage (Job A). Because Jobs B, D and G all follow Job A, they can all be carried out simultaneously.

Next, the information in the final two columns of the table is used to construct a network diagram.

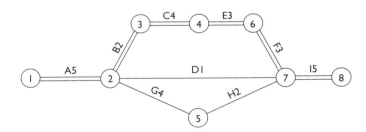

Here, the lines represent the jobs, indicated as the job letter followed by the estimated time. The nodes (circles) are numbered for clarity, and for use when a computer program is employed.

If you follow the lines from ① to ⑧ in this example, you will see that there are three possible routes.

- ①, ②, ③, ④, ⑥, ⑦, ⑧ = A5 + B2 + C4 + E3 + F3 + I5: total 22 days;
- ①, ②, ⑦, ⑧ = A5 + D1 + I5: total 11 days;
- ①, ②, ⑤, ⑦, ⑧ = A5 + G4 + H2 + I5: total 16 days.

The longest path is the first one (22 days), and this is called the **critical path**. (It is indicated by the double lines in the figure.) Any delay to the activities on this path will delay the whole project. But the other paths are not critical in this sense: even an extra ten days on the delivery of the machine, for example, would not hold up the project.

You can see how useful CPM is. In constructing the table and diagram, the planner is forced to think clearly and carefully about all activities during the planning stage. Then, once the diagram is drawn, the planner knows exactly where to concentrate the team's effort.

Activity 44

2 mins

Look back to the last diagram. Suppose it became possible to reduce the time to complete the path between nodes ②, ③, ④, ⑥, ⑦, by seven days. What effect would this have on:

a the critical path;

_____

_____

b the focus of the team's efforts?

_____

_____

Because the total number of days for the path ①, ②, ③, ④, ⑥, ⑦, ⑧ is now 22 − 7 = 15, it is no longer the critical path. Instead, the route ①, ②, ⑤, ⑦, ⑧ becomes the critical path, and more effort would be put into running services to the site and connecting them.

The first CPM diagram is based on estimated times. As actual times become known, the diagram should be redrawn to reflect the new situation. When this is done it, too, can sometimes indicate that the major effort of the team must be switched to a new area, because the critical path has changed.

5.6 Planning where the work will be done

For some projects, the location of the work is determined by the project objectives. The re-siting of a machine in the last example is a case in point. But in other situations, where the team works is a matter to consider carefully.

For one thing, it is beneficial if the team members are in close contact with one another. Jack Morton, a former head of Bell Telephones, suggested that two people who must collaborate to produce a result have between them barriers and bonds of two types: spatial and organizational. A spatial bond exists if they sit next to one another while working; if they are in different rooms, there is a spatial barrier. An organizational barrier is present if they each report to a different boss, or work in different departments. Morton said that a single barrier is acceptable, but a double barrier must never be permitted; this is known as **Morton's Rule**.

The ideal project team is one that is assigned full-time to one project manager, and in which everybody works together in the same place; this overcomes both types of barrier. Failing this, it is important that the members are either relocated so as to be together, or that they report to one leader, for the duration of the project.

As mentioned in Session C, another aspect of workspace is that it should be appropriate for the task. Any work area that is cramped, over-heated or under-heated, badly ventilated or otherwise poorly suited for human beings to be comfortable in, will reduce efficiency. To list a few examples:

- designers need well-lit offices;
- engineers need to be able to move around the machines they are working on;
- people expected to come up with ideas need to be isolated from distractions and noise;
- cooks and medical staff need hygienic conditions;
- everyone needs to feel safe and secure.

In this section, we have reviewed plans in terms of:

- deciding who does what (**who**);
- breaking a project into manageable jobs (**how**);
- timescales (**when**);
- location (**where**).

Now try the following Activity.

Activity 45

15 mins

Whether or not you are sometimes engaged in projects, tick the statements below that are valid for you.

	Always do well	Could do more effectively
I always encourage my team members to contribute to the planning of work.	☐	☐
My plans are always consistent with team objectives.	☐	☐
My plans are always realistic and achievable, within organizational constraints.	☐	☐
I always take account of the abilities and developmental needs of individuals when planning the allocation of work.	☐	☐
I always explain my plans to the team in sufficient detail, and at a level and pace appropriate to the needs of each individual.	☐	☐
I always take steps to confirm that individuals understand my plans.	☐	☐
I update my plans regularly, taking account of individual, team and organizational changes.	☐	☐

Now take at least **two** of the above activities in the above statements that you think you could do more effectively, and explain what actions you intend to take to improve your performance in this respect.

_____

_____

_____

_____

_____

_____

_____

_____

_____

During and after your next project, use the list to check your performance particularly in the areas you have highlighted for improvement. Make notes here.

_____

_____

_____

_____

_____

_____

_____

_____

_____

6 Project costs

All projects cost money. The financial aspects can be considered as three main activities:

- estimating the costs;
- setting budgets;
- keeping track of costs.

6.1 Estimating the costs

To get an accurate estimate of project costs, it will be necessary to list all the individual project jobs, all the materials, and all the equipment to be used.

Estimating costs is no trivial task for any project, so the first piece of advice might be summed up as: get any help you can find. You would normally:

- enlist the help of the team;
- call upon the expertise of individuals, groups and departments with specialized knowledge, whether or not they are assigned to the project.

Activity 46

In broad terms, which categories of expenditure do you think would be listed, when estimating the cost of a project? (One category would be labour costs, for example.)

_____

_____

_____

_____

_____

_____

_____

_____

_____

_____

_____

The components of cost will vary from one organization to another, but might be listed as follows.

■ Labour

the daily rate of pay for each team member, times the number of days he or she will work on the project.

■ Overheads

an agreed percentage of the labour costs, to cover items such as lighting, heating, insurance, and so on.

■ Materials

the costs of everything to be bought and used in the project, apart from capital equipment.

■ Equipment

the cost of buying or renting the plant and equipment needed.

■ Administration charges

an agreed percentage of the project costs, to be charged by other parts of the organization for services rendered, such as secretarial and accounting services.

For a project involving the manufacture of something, it may be necessary to break down each assembly to the level of discrete manufacturing operations or activities.

To take a simple example, if you were making a wooden table, you might need to list items such as those shown in the next chart.

For a project of a different kind, the following chart may not be suitable. If you were developing a new hairdressing salon, for example, you may decide to hire contractors to do all the work. In this case, your costs may simply consist of the fees for:

■ renting the premises;
■ designing the new layout;
■ refurbishing the premises;
■ purchasing chairs, mirrors, dryers and other equipment;
■ recruiting the staff; and so forth.

6.2 Setting budgets

The estimates produced before starting a project may be used to establish a **budget**. A budget is an itemized summary of expected expenditure and income, which is typically used to limit the amount spent on the project. The budget may be the most restrictive control imposed on the project team.

				Project: Table			
	LABOUR:				MATERIALS:		
No.	Activity	Estimated days	Actual days	Item	Qty	Unit price £	Total price £
01	cutting top to size			Wood: 1.2 × 0.9 m	1		
02	planning top			Wood: 0.075 × 0.075 m	4		
03	turning legs						
04	making joints						
05	gluing joints						
06	fitting legs						
07	varnishing and polishing			Total			£

			EQUIPMENT	
Total labour: ____ days @ £ ___ per day:	£	Hire of lathe		£
Overheads @ ____ %	£	Hire of plane		£
Materials:	£			
Equipment:	£			
Admin costs @ ___ %	£			
ESTIMATED TOTAL PROJECT COST:	£		Total	£

6.3 Keeping track of costs

Most project teams work to a budget, so they know they must not spend more than a certain sum over the period of the project.

Activity 47 · 3 mins

From your own experience, note **two** problems a project team may encounter, when trying to keep track of costs during the project.

_____

_____

_____

_____

The main difficulty is knowing whether progress is keeping pace with spending, and include the following problems.

■ Possible delays between making a payment and the amount appearing in the project records.

For any project, especially a large complicated one, strict record-keeping is essential. This is made easier if you are using a computer to log your activities and expenditure.

■ Estimates turning out to be wrong: for example, the design phase of a project may take much longer than anticipated.

It is always important to allow for contingencies when preparing estimates, perhaps in the form of an extra percentage of the costs.

■ Having many project activities going on at the same time, none of which are completed, making assessment of overall progress very hard to determine.

Some measure of achievement must be agreed for each type of work. This might be in terms of, say: the number of bricks laid as a proportion of the total; the percentage of training days completed; and so on.

> We do not have the space to consider all possible problems for all kinds of projects, even if that were possible. All project managers need to:
>
> ■ take time and trouble to get a firm grasp of what is to be done, and how it is to be achieved, before any other work commences;
> ■ be prepared for the unexpected;
> ■ keep records of every aspect of the project, and make regular progress reports;
> ■ call upon all the expert help and resources available.

If you want to find out more about how to control costs, you may like to study the workbook *Costs and Budgets* in this series. See the list at the back of this workbook.

Self-assessment 4

20 mins

1 What are the three constraints imposed on all projects?

_____

_____

2 What is 'storming'?

_____

_____

_____

3 What is the purpose of critical path analysis?

_____

_____

_____

_____

_____

4 What is Morton's Rule?

_____

_____

_____

5 What five components make up project costs?

_____

_____

_____

Answers can be found on pages 116–17.

7 Summary

- A **project** is an undertaking of work that has a definite beginning and a definite end. Typically, **resources** – people, materials, workspace and so on – are assigned for a **limited period** in order to achieve **defined objectives**.

- **Project constraints** are related to:

  - **costs**, which determine the amount of resources available;
  - **time**, which is seldom in sufficient supply;
  - **quality**, which involves all the characteristics of the project outcome.

- Before a project starts, a **feasibility study** may be set up. Such a study will look into all aspects of the proposal, by making costs calculations, identifying possible problems, and attempting to predict what will happen if the project goes ahead.

- Once the decision is made to go ahead with the project, the team will need to:

  - discuss the project at length;
  - gather information;
  - clarify the objectives;
  - look to similar earlier projects;
  - know what the constraints are;
  - identify individual team members' knowledge and experience.

- Most teams go through a **storming phase** when first formed.

- The **critical path method (CPM)** forces the team to think clearly and carefully about all activities, and helps to identify those activities that deserve the most concentrated effort.

- **Morton's Rule** states that both a spatial barrier and an organizational barrier must never be permitted.

- All projects cost money. We looked at:

  - estimating the costs;
  - setting budgets;
  - keeping track of costs.

Performance checks

1 Quick quiz

Jot down the answers to the following questions on *Planning to Work Efficiently*.

Question 1   What three kinds of transformations did we identify?

_____

_____

_____

Question 2   What **four** main types of resource did we identify?

_____

_____

_____

_____

Question 3   Define 'efficiency'.

_____

_____

Question 4   Explain the link between effectiveness and organizational objectives.

_____

_____

Question 5   Express, in your own words, the meaning of 'quality'.

_____

_____

Question 6   What's the main difference between a closed loop system and an open loop system?

_____

_____

_____

Question 7   What are the first **two** stages to be carried out, when controlling work?

_____

_____

_____

Question 8   Which **six** small words are so useful when forming a plan?

_____

_____

_____

Question 9   An important stage of work control is comparing performance against standards. Why should this activity not be done too frequently, and why should it not be done too infrequently?

_____

_____

_____

Question 10   Why is it so important that performance standards are well defined and expressly stated?

_____

_____

_____

Question 11   List **four** major areas of responsibility that a first line manager will have for materials.

_____

_____

_____

_____

Question 12   How can a materials variance report be useful in keeping track of materials?

_____
_____
_____

Question 13   What do we mean by an organization's quality system?

_____
_____
_____

Question 14   Under which **three** general headings do project constraints fall?

_____
_____
_____

Question 15   What do we mean by a feasibility study?

_____
_____
_____

Question 16   Explain briefly what you understand by the term 'storming', in relation to team formation.

_____
_____
_____

Question 17   Note **two** advantages of the critical path method (CPM).

_____
_____
_____

Question 18   Why is it helpful for a project if the team members are assigned full-time to one project manager, and that they all work together in the same place?

_____
_____
_____

Question 19   What is a budget, and why is it important for project leaders?

_____

_____

_____

Answers to these questions can be found on pages 118–19.

2 Workbook assessment

Read the following case incident and then deal with the questions that follow. Write your answers on a separate sheet of paper.

> For five years, Denny Shakur had been in charge of the administration office of a large mail order company. She was good at her job, and was well liked by both her workteam and her manager. However, in a recent audit by the firm's external accountants, her section and team were criticized heavily. A report indicated that Denny had become sloppy about overtime and the use of operating supplies (that is, stationery, blank forms, and so on), and had allowed the misuse of telephones and copying equipment. It recommended that Denny be issued a budget for these items, and that her manager initiate tighter controls.

1   Describe how Denny needs to apply the following **four** stages of control to the work she is responsible for:

   ■ setting performance standards;
   ■ collecting data to measure performance;
   ■ comparing results with standards;
   ■ taking corrective action.

2   Denny would have to develop standards of her own to meet her overall budgeted target. Suggest at least **one** way she might do this.

3   Design a document that would enable Denny to measure the performance with respect to a set standard for one activity in her department.

4   What might Denny do to encourage her team to respond positively to the criticism?

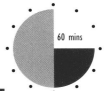

3 Work-based assignment

**S/NVQ
D6**

The time guide for this assignment gives you an approximate idea of how long it is likely to take you to write up your findings. You will find you need to spend some additional time gathering information, taking to colleagues and thinking about the assignment.

Your written response to this assignment may form useful evidence for your S/NVQ portfolio. The assignment is designed to help you to demonstrate the following Personal Competences:

- building teams;
- focusing on results;
- thinking and taking decisions;
- striving for excellence.

**What you have
to do**

1 Think back to one project (large or small) that you have been involved in, either as leader or team member. First of all, describe the project in terms of the following stages. Do not spend too long on the first part of this exercise; it is mainly aimed at making you consider what you learned. The questions are intended as prompts: you do not necessarily have to answer every one. The stages are as follows.

- Defining objectives.

   What were the objectives of the project? Who defined them? To what extent were they eventually achieved?

- Making a plan.

   How would you summarize the plan, briefly? Who took part in preparing the plan?

- Communication of the plan within the team.

   How was the plan communicated? How well was it communicated?

- Setting performance standards.

  What standards were set or implied? Who set them?

- Collecting data to measure progress.

  What data was collected? How well was it collected?

- Comparing results with standards and objectives.

  How was the comparison made, to check whether the project was on track?

- Taking corrective action to modify the plan if necessary.

  What corrective actions were taken?

2   Now decide what you will do differently if you are put in charge of a project. Go through each of the stages again, and write down in some detail what your approach to the task will be, and how you will ensure that fewer mistakes are made. Make any assumptions you like about the kind of project it will be; if you know of a forthcoming project, so much the better.

Reflect and review

1 Reflect and review

Now that you have completed your work on *Planning to work Efficiently*, let us review our workbook objectives.

■ You should be better able to recognize what efficiency means, in the context of your workplace.

Defining the word 'efficiency' is not difficult. The definition we used was:'making the best use of resources, to achieve production of goods or services'. What is more relevant is how **you** view efficiency, now that you have finished the workbook, in relation to **your** resources and work processes.

Try to explain what you have learned, by answering the following questions.

■ What inefficiencies have I identified in the way I and my team operate?

_____

_____

_____

■ What are the effects of these inefficiencies on the organization as a whole?

_____

_____

_____

■ You should be better able to identify the stages involved in planning and controlling work, and apply them to your own environment.

As we have discussed, there are seven stages that are all fundamental to the control work, of whatever kind.

1 Define objectives.
2 Make a plan.

3 Communicate the plan within the team.
4 Set performance standards.
5 Collect data to measure progress.
6 Compare results with standards and objectives.
7 Take corrective action to modify the plan if necessary.

If one stage is done badly, or missed out, the chances of success tend to diminish.

■ Briefly explain how you could apply one of the seven stages to the work you are currently doing.

_____

_____

_____

■ You should be better able to control the resources available to you and your team.

If we include your team in the resources available to you, then you may consider that your job consists almost entirely of controlling resources.

In session C, we reviewed some resources: materials, plant and equipment, and people; together with quality, work flow, and work methods. We discussed four major areas of responsibility when controlling materials: receiving, handling, processing, and storage.

On the vitally important subject of quality, we noted that the quality of a product or service is a reflection of the way the producer or supplier is organized and managed. One quality systems standard, BS EN ISO 9000:2000, sets out a number of steps or elements that define what organizations have to do to set up and maintain an adequate quality system.

Maintenance, another key subject, was discussed. As you will be aware, first line managers have responsibilities for making sure that equipment under their control is properly maintained.

The control of work flow may be assisted by the use of charts such as Gantt charts, upon which work schedules can be set out.

■ Which of these subjects discussed in session C is your weakest area of management, and which the strongest?

_____

_____

_____

_____

■ How will you set about taking actions to improve your skills and knowledge in your weakest area of expertise?

_____

_____

_____

_____

■ You should be better able to recognize the importance of setting, and checking against, agreed standards.

Standards was a recurring theme in this workbook. Let's remind ourselves of some of the points made.

1 To control something, you need to have some way of knowing when the process is going as you want it to. The way you do this is to compare results and performance against a standard. This standard may be in your head, or it may be a measurable quantity. But without having a standard, you can't control anything.

2 The organization needs to be sure that its standards are at least as high as the customer's standards.

3 To be meaningful, standards need to be expressed very clearly and should preferably be measurable.

4 Comparing performance against standards too frequently involves unnecessary expense and work for no real return. Too infrequent comparisons can mean that danger signals are missed, which may result in losses in productivity and output.

5 The standard for a particular commodity or service must be written down in such a way that it is clear exactly what criteria the product must meet. This is necessary so that any differences between the standard and the product can be assessed, and, if necessary, corrected.

6 Every organization needs to have a well-defined quality system that can ensure products meet an agreed standard of quality consistently.

7 The international quality system standard BS EN ISO 9000:2000 sets out a number of steps or elements that define what organizations have to do to set up and maintain an adequate quality system.

8 In every decision you make you are defining standards.

■ How well do you recognize and acknowledge the standards you and your team work to? Could you write them all down, if you had to?

_____

_____

_____

■ Are you satisfied that the standards you and others set are not too low, and not too high? If not, what actions might you take to review these standards?

_____

_____

_____

The last objective was as follows.

■ You should be better able to contribute to the planning and control of projects.

A project is a 'bounded' undertaking, in that it is planned to last for a limited time period, and typically has resources assigned to it temporarily.

Planning and controlling projects is not very different from managing other kinds of activities, because the same principles apply. The seven stages we listed earlier are all relevant to project management.

We looked at some specific techniques, notably the use of Gantt charts for task scheduling, the critical path method (CPM) for determining which activities deserve the primary focus, and cost estimation.

■ Do you need to learn more about project management or about specific techniques? How will you set about finding out?

_____

_____

_____

2 Action plan

Use this plan to further develop for yourself a course of action you want to take. Make a note in the left-hand column of the issues or problems you want to tackle, and then decide what you intend to do, and make a note in column 2.

Desired outcomes			
1 Issues	2 Action	3 Resources	4 Target completion
Actual outcomes			

The resources you need might include time, materials, information or money. You may need to negotiate for some of them, but they could be something easily acquired, like half an hour of somebody's time, or a chapter of a book. Put whatever you need in column 3. No plan means anything without a timescale, so put a realistic target completion date in column 4.

Finally, describe the outcome you want to achieve as a result of this plan, whether it is for your own benefit or advancement, or a more efficient way of doing things.

▪ 3 Extensions

Extension 1

Book	*Introduction to Operations Management*
Author	John Naylor
Edition	2002
Publisher	Prentice Hall
ISBN	0 2736 5578 7

This book covers a number of the subjects of this workbook, including efficiency and effectiveness, transformation processes, work study, bench-marking, Total Quality Management, and continuous improvement. Particular chapters relevant to our subject are: Chapter 6 – Studying work; Chapter 8 – Facility layout: manufacture and isolated service; Chapter 9 – Facility layout: personal and self service.

As the Preface says: 'This book gives a comprehensive coverage of operations management for those who come to the subject for the first time.'

Extension 2

Book	*Production Planning and Control*
Author	W. Bolton
Edition	1994
Publisher	Longman Scientific and Technical

This book is described as aiming 'to give the student a practical and comprehensive appreciation and understanding of: the ways in which manufacturing companies are organized; the nature and diversity of engineering products; the organization of production; the planning and control of production'.

Extension 3

Book	*The Project Management Pocketbook*
Author	Mike Applegarth and Keith Posner
Edition	1998
Publisher	Management Pocketbooks

Book   *Successful Project Management*
Author   Trevor L. Young
Edition   2000
Publisher Kogan Page in association with *The Sunday Times*

These Extensions can be taken up via your ILM Centre. They will either have them or will arrange that you have access to them. However, it may be more convenient to check out the materials with your personnel or training people at work – they may well give you access. There are other good reasons for approaching your own people; for example, they will become aware of your interest and you can involve them in your development.

4 Answers to self-assessment questions

**Self-assessment 1
on pages 21–2**

1   The completed diagram is:

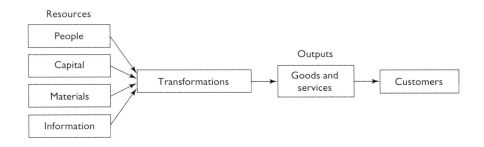

2   Compare your responses with the answer given below.

Transformation type	Sector			
	Manufacturing	Transport	Supply	Service
Improving	f	b	b	c, e
Caretaking	f	b	b	e
Transferring		a, b	a, b, d	

There may be some here which you disagree with.

(a) The regional electricity company transfers electricity from the National Grid to its customers. It is therefore in the transport and supply business. There is a case for putting it into the service sector, and you might say that it 'transports' electricity, by providing electricity cables.

(b) A water company has to purify (i.e. improve) and take care of water, and also transfer it to customers. It is in both the transport and supply business. Again, it might see itself as also providing a service.

(c) A hairdresser simply provides a hair-improving service.

(d) A hardware shop supplies goods to its customers, but does not improve them or take care of them (except in an incidental way). The shop may also pride itself on the good service it gives.

(e) A residential school improves and takes care of children, but does not supply, transport or manufacture them!

(f) A farm is a manufacturer, improving, and taking care of crops and farm animals and their products.

3 (a) EFFICIENCY means making the best use of RESOURCES, to achieve production of goods or SERVICES.

(b) Work organizations TRANSFORM resources (capital, materials and INFORMATION, with the help of PEOPLE) into goods and services, which are provided to their CUSTOMERS.

(c) QUALITY can be defined as all the FEATURES and characteristics of a product or service that affect its ability to SATISFY the needs of customers and USERS.

(d) For information to be valid and reliable it must be ACCURATE and complete.

Self-assessment 2 on pages 46–8

1 The completed diagram is shown below.

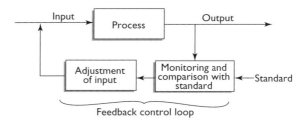

Feedback control loop

2 You cannot achieve your objectives, or even know if you are nearing your objectives, if don't know what your objectives are.

3 ■ All systems are controlled by setting a desired standard, and comparing results *against this standard*.

- Closed loop systems have feedback, monitoring and control, but *open loop systems do not.*
- Clear objectives are *necessary for good control.*
- Performance standards should be *well defined and expressly stated.*
- The big mistake is to assume that you don't need a plan, *because you think the what, why, who, how, when and where are all too self-evident.*
- The cost and effort of monitoring has to be balanced *against the improvement in control that it can bring.*

4   a is a project or team objective.
    b is a task objective.
    c is an organizational objective.
    d is a mission statement.

5   The corrected statements are as follows. The actual wording may differ from yours.

   a Everything you do takes up your time, *so you shouldn't check anything unnecessarily frequently.*
   b You need to assess performance after you've had enough time to study it, *but before it becomes too late to take corrective action.*
   c Once a standard is set, it *may be necessary to allow for some deviation from it.*
   d To be meaningful, standards need to be expressed very clearly and preferably *should be measurable.*
   e The best way to communicate with the team is to give *information at a pace and level that each individual can deal with.*
   f Plans need to cover all the people within your area of responsibility, be realistic and achievable, and take account of the *abilities of your team, and their need to develop their skills.*
   g A plan is *a detailed scheme for attaining an objective.*
   h The process of comparison should be quite straightforward, provided that work objectives are *well defined,* measurement of results is *accurate* and performance standards are *clear and precise.*

Self-assessment 3 on pages 75–6	I	**Problem**		**Possible solution**
		a A delay is caused because materials are not available when and where they are needed.	ii	Ensure that materials are ordered in sufficient quantities, and to the correct specification.
		b Materials are wastefully used.	vi	Improve work methods to make more efficient use of materials.
		c Materials are found to be damaged when they are about to be used.	i	Improve handling methods.

d Materials are found to be of the wrong type, just when they are about to be used.

   v Improve ordering and goods receiving procedures.

e Too much of one kind of material is in stock, and too little of another kind.

   iii Monitor the consumption rate of each type of material more carefully.

f Pilfering of materials occurs.

   iv Increase security in the stores area.

2 a Documented quality policy

   vii Must be read and understood by all employees, and contains an organization chart showing who is responsible for what.

b Quality manual

   viii Sets out all the procedures for implementing the system.

c Quality

   iii All the characteristics of a product or service.

d Quality system

   vi Ensures that products are made or delivered to the right level of quality in the first place.

e Ability to achieve quality

   ii Know-how and training which enable quality goals to be translated into quality work.

f Commitment to quality

   i The dedication and determination that people need in order to bring quality of work to a high standard and to keep it there.

g Communication

   v The link between those who set the standards and those who have to interpret them, and between those who do the work and those who measure the results.

h Attention to detail

   iv The difference between having good intentions about quality and actually achieving results.

Self-assessment 4 on pages 98–9

1 The three constraints on all projects are costs, time and quality.

2 'Storming' is the phase of uncertainty which new teams go through as they find their feet within the group.

3 Critical path analysis is a tool for planning project timescales. All tasks in the project are listed in a table, together with the time they will take to complete, and the tasks that will precede and follow them. The information is then used to construct a network diagram. This identifies the critical path containing the activities that, if they are delayed, will affect the whole project schedule.

4 Morton's Rule states that people who work in collaboration need two types of bond between them – spacial and organizational. If there is a barrier to one type of bond, the collaboration can still work. If there are barriers to both, it won't.

5 The five components of project costs are labour, overheads, materials, equipment and administration charges.

5 Answers to activities

Activity 3 on page 6

You may have noted as people your own work team, or included other departments such as sales, accounts, shop staff, operators, and so on.

Capital could be the building you work in, the equipment you use in your job, the budgets you work to, or the ground you stand on.

The materials you listed will depend on the kind of work you do; they might be made from paper, metal, plastic, ceramics, etc. You may have included gas, electricity or oil as energy consumed.

Information could be in the form of specifications, job descriptions, formulations, reports, and so on.

Activity 6 on page 11

Other examples of inefficiency might include:

■ using unskilled labour, which may result in need for reworking and a return to the transformation stage
■ poor transformation processes, which result in waste and low quality outputs.

Other examples of ineffectiveness might include:

■ not agreeing what the objectives are or having no clear objectives to aim for – all parts of the model would be adversely affected
■ too many resources being used to return minimal profit through low sales.

6 Answers to the quick quiz

Answer 1   The three transformation types were improving, caretaking and transferring.

Answer 2   The four resource types were people, capital, materials and information.

Answer 3   We defined efficiency as 'making the best use of resources, to achieve production of goods and services'.

Answer 4   One way of expressing this relationship is to say that, to be effective, an organization, individual or group has to achieve agreed objectives.

Answer 5   Quality can be defined as all the features and characteristics of a product or service which affect its ability to satisfy the needs of customers and users.

Answer 6   Closed loop systems have feedback, monitoring and control; open loop systems do not.

Answer 7   The first two stages are: define your objectives and make a plan.

Answer 8   The six words are: what, why, when, where, how and why.

Answer 9   Comparing performance against standards too **frequently** involves unnecessary expense and work for no real return. Too **infrequent** comparisons can mean that danger signals are missed, which may result in losses in productivity and output.

Answer 10   A performance standard is something you measure or assess performance by. To do this, you need to know, as precisely as possible, what the standard is.

Answer 11   We considered: receiving; handling; processing; storing.

Answer 12   The variance report gives the manager an opportunity to check the accuracy of forecasts, and to identify major variances in the use of materials, so that corrective action can be taken.

Answer 13   An organization's quality system can be defined as 'the organizational structure, responsibilities, procedures, processes and resources for implementing quality management'. You may have expressed this in another way.

Answer 14   Project constraints are related to: costs, which determine the amount of resources available; time, which is seldom in sufficient supply; and quality, which involves all the characteristics of the project outcome.

Answer 15   A feasibility study is a preliminary evaluation of all aspects of a project proposal, in which costs are calculated, possible problems identified and a prediction made about what will happen if the project goes ahead.

Answer 16   Storming is a period of conflict, which may occur soon after a team is formed. It is characterized by friction of various kinds, and is symptomatic of the team members getting to know what to expect, and what is expected of them.

Answer 17   In constructing a CPM diagram, the planner is forced to think clearly and carefully about all activities during the planning stage. Then, once the diagram is drawn, the planner knows exactly where to concentrate the team's effort.

Answer 18   This overcomes two kinds of barrier: a barrier of space, which exists if people don't work close to one another, and a barrier of organization, which can exist if they work for different managers.

Answer 19   A budget is an itemized summary of expected expenditure and income, which is typically used to limit the amount spent on a project. The budget may be the most restrictive control imposed in the project team.

6 Certificate

Completion of this certificate by an authorized person shows that you have worked through all the parts of this workbook and satisfactorily completed the assessments. The certificate provides a record of what you have done that may be used for exemptions or as evidence of prior learning against other nationally certificated qualifications.

superseries

Planning to Work Efficiently

....

has satisfactorily completed this workbook

Name of signatory ....

Position ....

Signature ....

Date ....

Official stamp

Pergamon
Flexible
Learning

Fifth Edition

superseries

FIFTH EDITION

Workbooks in the series:

For prices and availability please telephone our order helpline
or email

+44 (0) 1865 474010
directorders@elsevier.com